JODI A. MINDELL, PHD, is the author of *Take Charge of Your Child's Sleep: The All-in-One Resource for Solving Sleep Problems in Kids and Teens* and *Sleeping Through the Night: How Infants, Toddlers, and Their Parents Can Get a Good Night's Sleep.* She is the associate director of the Sleep Center at the Children's Hospital of Philadelphia and professor of psychology at Saint Joseph's University.

From Pregnancy to
Early Motherhood—
Helping You and Your Baby
Sleep Through the Night

Sleep
Deprived
No More

Jodi A. Mindell, PhD

MARLOWE & COMPANY
NEW YORK

To Scott and Caelie, as always

Contents

Acknowledgments

My deepest appreciation goes to those who continue to support my endeavors to educate the world about sleep: my agent, Carol Mann, and my editor, Katie McHugh, for believing in this project; Mark Turner, my all-time champion; Emily Miles Terry, Leslie Rossman, and Linda Phelan of Open Book Publicity; all of the hardworking folks at Johnson's Baby who support my dream to get the word out about sleep, including Lorena Telofski, Kate Luedtke, Ben Wiegand, Ellen Kurtz, Brian Gartside and my colleagues in the Department of Psychology at Saint Joseph's University and in the Sleep Center at the Children's Hospital of Philadelphia, as well as all of my colleagues in the world of pediatric sleep, including Judy Owens, Lisa Meltzer, Avi Sadeh, and Mary Carskadon.

Huge thanks go to all of my friends and relatives who have been there throughout the years, especially my parents, who continue to provide all their support and encouragement. But my biggest thank-you continues to go to my two favorite people in the whole world: my husband and biggest supporter, Scott McRobert, since none of what I do would be possible without him; and my daughter, Caelie, who continues to be the center of our universe and who luckily doesn't mind that her mom travels all the time and who loves her "daddy-daughter days."

PART I

An Introduction to Sleep

ONE

Sleep Deprived No More

"To sleep, perchance to dream—ay, there's the rub."
—*Shakespeare,* from Hamlet

Ahhh, to sleep! Doesn't that sound glorious? There is nothing better than crawling into bed after a long day and falling into a deep sleep, not waking until the next morning. Unfortunately, blissful sleep may be just a fond memory. Now that you are pregnant or a new mom, sleep may not be as simple or as easy as it used to be.

Most pregnant women struggle with sleep problems. And these problems don't just start in the third trimester. Rather, thanks to surging hormones, sleep disturbances may begin right at the start of pregnancy. That means that you may experience nine long months of problems sleeping. And unfortunately, obstetricians and other health care providers often ignore sleep problems. Pregnant women are frequently told that it is just part of pregnancy and they must deal with it. Usually the most sympathy they receive is a comment from friends and family: "Just wait until you have the baby, then you'll know what lack of sleep means."

Once the baby arrives, expect less sleep, at least for the first few months. Your baby is going to be up during the night, especially in the first month or two, and yes, there are sure to be some tough days. After that, your baby's sleep schedule will start to become more predictable and everyone in the house will start getting more sleep. However, heading back to work, taking care of other children, and life's ups and downs can all contribute to continued sleep issues.

Luckily, however, even during pregnancy and post-baby, sleep *is* possible. You don't have to suffer through countless sleepless nights and spend your waking moments feeling totally sleep deprived. This book will show you many things that you can do to get the sleep you need so that you can fully experience the wondrous moments of pregnancy and your brand-new baby.

Common Sleep Issues Faced by Pregnant Women and New Moms

SLEEP ISSUES ARE almost universal! Look left. Look right. If you see a pregnant woman or a new mom, chances are that she's experiencing some type of sleep struggle, whether just waking up for a quick trip to the bathroom or experiencing prolonged sleepless nights. The National Sleep Foundation's *Sleep in America Poll 2007* surveyed women of all ages and found that pregnant women and new moms were especially likely to experience sleep problems.

	Pregnant Women	New Moms
Report that they rarely or never get a good night's sleep	30%	42%
Experience insomnia at least a few nights a week	84%	84%
Snore	27%	29%
Have restless legs syndrome	21%	8%
Nap at least twice a week	54%	40%
Have driven drowsy at least once a month	31%	38%

Pregnancy

In addition to the above findings by the National Sleep Foundation, a study that we conducted in my lab on sleep during pregnancy found that 97 percent of pregnant women fail to sleep through the night by the end of their pregnancy and 92 percent sleep restlessly. So just about every pregnant woman faces some kind of sleep issue. Just because sleep problems are typical during pregnancy, however, doesn't mean that you can't do anything about them. Your sleep may never be perfect while you are pregnant, but there are many things that you can do to improve it as much as possible. That is what this book is about: helping you sleep better so that you can feel your best.

New Moms

Similarly, new moms are not getting the sleep they need. A majority of new moms do not get enough sleep at night, and most say they don't get a good night's sleep most nights. Some of these sleep issues are related to being up with the baby during the night, but another portion are due to poor sleep habits and other common sleep disrupters. Again, this book is here to help.

How Much Sleep Do You Need?

THE AVERAGE ADULT needs 8 hours of sleep. Actually, studies indicate that it is really 8.2 hours (8 hours and 14 minutes). This number comes from classic studies in which adult volunteers stayed in caves for weeks at a time. All of the adults ended up getting 8.2 hours of sleep every night. There are some individual differences, so we typically recommend that adults need between 7 and 9 hours of sleep at night. That's right, there are just as many people who need less than 8 hours of sleep at night as there are who need more than 8 hours.

Interestingly, recent research seems to show that there really aren't that many individual differences in sleep need. Rather, it indicates that there are individual differences in how well people tolerate being sleep deprived. That is, *everyone* needs about 8 hours of sleep, but some women have an easier time getting by on 5 or 6 hours than others. Unfortunately, there is no way to train your body to handle being sleep deprived. You can either tolerate it or not. Figuring out whether you are one of these people, though, will help you determine the minimum number of hours of sleep that you need (see quiz, pages 8–9).

How Much Sleep Are Pregnant and New Moms Actually Getting?

ONE QUESTION THAT often is asked is how much sleep women really get when they are pregnant and after the baby is born. One study surveyed women before they were pregnant, during their pregnancy, and then in the three months after their delivery. Below are some of the results of this study.

	Before pregnancy	1st trimester	2nd trimester	3rd trimester	New moms
Hours of nighttime sleep	7.8	8.2	8.0	7.8	7.0
Hours of total sleep (nighttime and naps)	8.0	8.7	8.4	8.3	7.0
Snoring	5.0%	6.8%	6.8%	10.4%	4.4%
Percentage reporting awakening at night	72.8%	92.2%	94.5%	98.1%	96.3%

In general, this study found that pregnant women are actually getting, and likely needing, more sleep during pregnancy, but that amount drops greatly after the baby is born. In addition, sleep problems are much more common during pregnancy. Some of these sleep problems, like snoring, are specific to pregnancy, whereas others, such as waking at night, become almost universal for both pregnant women and new moms.

Older Pregnant Women Sleep Less

Another interesting finding in this study was that pregnant women over the age of 35 spent the least amount of time in bed, had the shortest amount of total sleep, and woke up earliest in the morning, compared to younger pregnant women. Why is that? It seems that older women are more likely to have established careers, are more likely to be working throughout their pregnancy, and spend less time in bed. All of these factors lead to less sleep overall. Women over 35 should keep this in mind. Adjust your schedule to maximize how much sleep you get, being sure to go to bed early and not wake up too early.

It's Harder the First Time Around

Patricia was pregnant with her second child and was exhausted, especially after running around with her 2-year-old all day. She usually headed to bed soon after tucking in her daughter.

In addition, for some reason, sleep is much more problematic for women the first time around. Contrary to what you might expect, women who are pregnant with their first baby get less sleep at night than women who are pregnant with their second, third, or fourth child. This trend continues once the baby is born. At one month after the birth of a baby, women with more than one child sleep much better at night than women who just had their first baby.

This difference is likely related to a change in priorities and even a change in identity. Women pregnant for the first time are not yet in "mommy mode" and may not have changed their lifestyle yet to reflect this change in status. They may still be working longer hours, staying up later at night, and haven't yet changed their schedules and expectations to be more baby and kid friendly.

Quiz

Are You Getting Enough Sleep?

TO FIGURE OUT if you are getting enough sleep and functioning at your best, take the following test.

Consider the past week or two and answer true or false to the following statements.

1. When I wake up in the morning, I feel groggy.
2. I fall asleep at night in less than 5 minutes.

3. I could fall asleep at any time.
4. I have fallen asleep at a time when I shouldn't have, such as while driving or talking on the phone.
5. I often fall asleep in the evening while watching television or reading (not while in bed).
6. I nap most days.
7. I become drowsy when doing repetitive tasks.

If you answered true to two or more of the above statements, you are probably not getting enough sleep.

Why Sleep Matters

Michelle, mom of 10-month-old Alex, asked only one thing of her husband for Mother's Day—a night in a hotel room all by herself so that she could sleep!

LIKE MICHELLE, THERE are many new moms who crave a good night's sleep. If you are at the point where your greatest wish in life is one night of sleep, then you need to do something about it. So get that hotel room or spend the night at your mom's or best friend's house. Put your husband on baby duty for a night and go sleep elsewhere in the house. You are not helping anyone by walking around feeling like a zombie.

A great deal of research has focused on the impact of not getting enough sleep. Overall, and not surprisingly, we know that being sleep deprived can affect every aspect of your life. Studies have shown that it affects your mood, your performance, your parenting ability, your health, and your satisfaction with your relationship. In addition, being sleep deprived can have danger-ous consequences.

Mood

Dawn, mom of 8-month-old Jack, was at the point where she was so tired that she just didn't care anymore. She was also grumpy all the time and felt like she never laughed anymore.

Not getting enough sleep will make you feel irritable and cranky. You may be much quicker to get frustrated and angry, whether at your husband, your children, your boss, or even your poor dog. Some women report that they get mean when they don't get enough sleep. And others find that they become indifferent (a general feeling of "who cares," or as your local teen would say, "whatever").

Cognitive Ability

You literally cannot think as well if you don't get enough sleep. Lack of sleep affects every aspect of cognitive ability, including attention, memory, decision making, and problem solving. You may be forgetful, not able to make a decision, and basically not able to think clearly.

Diane, a 32-year-old new mom, literally spent 15 minutes sitting in her car searching for her glasses. She looked everywhere—dumping her purse, emptying out the diaper bag, and searching under every seat in the car. She knew she wasn't getting enough sleep when she finally realized that they were perched on top of her head the entire time.

Similarly, Courtney couldn't find her car keys anywhere. She knew that the last time she had them was in the morning when she went to the grocery store. After an hour of searching the entire house, the only thing she could figure out that may have happened was that she locked her keys in her car. She finally called her local garage to come and break into her car. Thirty minutes later they had the car open, but no keys to be found. Later that night, Courtney found her keys in the refrigerator. She was mortified.

Performance

No matter your gender or age, pregnant or not, being sleep deprived means that you are not going to do things as well. Your reaction time slows down and your performance can decrease. Many women report making more mistakes at work and not being able to do the simplest tasks.

Caroline, mom to 3-year-old Lindsay and 7-month-old Grace, was making mistakes at work that she had never made before. Letters were going out with the wrong addresses, she lost several important files, and she completely forgot to show up at a meeting with a major client. She was so exhausted all the time that she just couldn't get her brain to function as usual.

It is often these small lapses that you may notice when you are not getting enough sleep. Worryingly, sleep deprivation can lead to bigger errors. There have been several major disasters in which sleep deprivation has been implicated as playing a role, including the *Exxon Valdez* oil spill, the nuclear meltdown at Chernobyl, and the explosion of the space shuttle *Challenger*. Fortunately, the impact of being sleep deprived is not permanent. Get a few solid nights of sleep and you'll be back to your usual self.

Health

Yes, what your grandmother always said is likely true. If you don't get enough sleep, you are more likely to get sick. Whether it's a cold, the flu, or something more serious, your immune system is not as good at fighting off illness if you don't get enough sleep. During sleep your body produces cytokines, which help the immune system fight infections. Lack of sleep not only affects how well your body fights off infections, it even affects how well your body produces antibodies after a vaccination. A recent study found that people who were sleep deprived produced less than half as many flu antibodies after receiving the flu vaccine. The result is that you are less protected later on when you are exposed to the flu.

Recent research has shown that being sleep deprived also affects more serious health issues, such as diabetes, obesity, and heart disease. For example, improved sleep can improve glucose control in those with diabetes; less sleep increases the risk for obesity; and sleep apnea can contribute to heart disease. Finally, we also know that lack of sleep makes accidental injuries more likely, such as falling or cutting yourself with a knife.

When Sondra was six months pregnant, she tripped over their dog, who was lying in the middle of the kitchen. The dog always lay down in the same spot, but on that day Sondra was just too tired to notice. Her baby was luckily unharmed, but Sondra ended up in a cast for six weeks. Getting around on crutches is hard enough, but doing so while pregnant is almost impossible!

Life Satisfaction

Lisa and Dan were arguing all the time. They argued over who should get up with the baby when she woke up, they argued over what to do when the baby woke up, and they argued over who was more tired. Basically, they argued over everything and anything. Fortunately, they were able to look back later and realize that their arguing was purely a result of exhaustion and frustration.

It's hard to be happy if you are sleepy and tired all the time. Being sleep deprived can lead to lower parenting satisfaction and marital satisfaction. Many couples report that not getting enough sleep as a result of their baby puts a strain on their relationship. Couples often argue about the best way to handle their baby's sleep, such as whether they should respond to their baby's cries. They also argue more in general, simply because they are so tired and they have less patience. Moms are also less happy as parents. It's hard to enjoy the baby when you are so tired that all you want to do is lie down and take a nap. You will also get more frustrated when your baby is crying for no apparent reason or when you're toddler asks "Why?" for the twentieth time in a row.

The good news, though, is that these same studies show that once everyone is getting some sleep, everything improves. Mom and Dad are happier, are getting along better, and are enjoying parenting. So work on getting the sleep that you need so that you can be alert, energetic, and enjoy life!

Postpartum Depression

Lucinda had no energy, was sad all the time, and just felt like crying. She had a wonderful husband, a beautiful 5-month-old baby (who

still woke up twice a night), and a great career. She didn't understand
why she was feeling so down.

Not getting adequate sleep has been implicated in the development of postpartum depression. Those women who do not get enough sleep at night are much more likely to feel depressed. Furthermore, sleep deprivation at the end of pregnancy and during the first few weeks after the birth of a baby predicts the later development of postpartum depression. A complete discussion of these topics appears later in chapter 10.

Alertness While Driving

Liz was scaring herself. She was 14 weeks pregnant and just so tired.
Every day at 1:00 p.m. she had to pick up her 4-year-old son from
camp. One day, she was so worried that she was going to fall asleep
at the wheel that she made her son talk to her the entire way home.
Liz realized that her sleepy driving was dangerous, so she decided to
begin carpooling with another mom. Liz would take both boys to camp
in the morning and her friend did afternoon pick-up.

One of the biggest concerns about being sleepy is driving drowsy. Did you know that drowsy driving causes more car accidents than driving while intoxicated? Approximately 60 percent of adults have driven drowsy in the past year, and one-third have literally fallen asleep at the wheel. The National Sleep Foundation's *Sleep in America Poll 2007* found that 31 percent of pregnant women and 38 percent of new moms have driven drowsy in the past month. Be careful! If you are not getting enough sleep, and especially if you feel sleepy, don't drive! Drowsy driving can have deadly consequences.

The frightening thing about drowsy driving is that most people are not able to tell when they are sleepy or are about to fall asleep while driving. We are notoriously bad at recognizing sleepiness in ourselves. Study after study has shown that during a driving simulation test, sleep-deprived adults will report that they are fine, but then fall asleep moments later.

Drowsy-driving accidents are more likely to occur in the middle of the night, as you might expect. But, surprisingly, the next most dangerous time is between three and five in the afternoon, when our bodies experience a natural circadian dip (meaning that we are likely to feel tired at this time of day). Turning up the radio or rolling down the car window to get a blast of fresh air is not going to prevent you from falling asleep at the wheel. Instead, the only thing that will counteract sleepiness is sleep.

If you are sleepy, be careful. Don't take long drives in the car (some moms and dads even fall asleep on short drives!). Stop and take a quick nap, even if just for ten to fifteen minutes. Figure out the limits of what you can reasonably and safely achieve.

Sleepiness can be dangerous in other situations too. Be careful in the kitchen and when doing other chores, such as yard work. Accidents can happen when you are tired. Often we are expected to get things done no matter how much sleep we got the previous night, week, or even month. Before you jump in and do whatever is expected, think about whether you realistically can. Will you be safe? Will you be endangering others?

. . .

Quiz

How Sleepy Are You?

THE EPWORTH SLEEPINESS Scale is the most widely used questionnaire to measure how sleepy a person is during the day. Complete the following questionnaire to assess your level of daytime sleepiness.

How likely are you to doze off or fall asleep in the following situations, in contrast to feeling just tired? This refers to your usual way of life in recent times. Even if you have not done some of these things recently, try to work out how they would have affected you. Use the following scale to choose the most appropriate number for each situation:

0 = no chance of dozing
1 = slight chance of dozing
2 = moderate chance of dozing
3 = high chance of dozing

SITUATION	CHANCE OF DOZING
Sitting and reading	_____
Watching TV	_____
Sitting inactive in a public place (e.g., a theater or a meeting)	_____
As a passenger in a car for an hour without a break	_____
Lying down to rest in the afternoon when circumstances permit	_____

SITUATION	CHANCE OF DOZING
Sitting and talking to someone	_____
Sitting quietly after a lunch without alcohol	_____
In a car, while stopped for a few minutes in traffic	_____

SCORING:

Add up your score and see how sleepy you are.

Score between 1 and 6	Congratulations, you are getting enough sleep!
Score between 7 and 9	Your score is average.
Score of 10 or higher	You are very sleepy during the day.

What You'll Learn in This Book

THIS BOOK PROVIDES practical advice and tips on how to help you and your baby get a good night's sleep. It will help you no longer feel as sleep deprived, from the moment that you find out that you are pregnant through the first six months after your baby is born.

The book is organized into four sections:

PART I (chapters 1 through 3) provides an introduction to sleep and sleep problems, a basic overview of sleep, and an essential review of good sleep habits that you should develop.

PART II (chapters 4 through 7) presents what you can expect in terms of sleep issues throughout the three trimesters of pregnancy. Sleep tips specific to each trimester are provided.

PART III (chapters 7 through 9) provides information on the most common sleep problems experienced by women during pregnancy and following the birth of their baby. Chapter 7 discusses insomnia and strategies to conquer sleepless nights. Chapter 8 discusses restless legs syndrome and periodic limb movement disorder, two related sleep disorders. And, finally, chapter 9 presents information on snoring and sleep apnea, two sleep problems that often develop during pregnancy.

PART IV (chapters 10 through 12) focuses on sleep after the baby is born, offering strategies to help both you and your baby sleep through the night. Chapter 10 helps Mom get the sleep she needs in the first six weeks after the baby is born. Additional information is provided on postpartum depression, managing sleep, and ways to share nighttime duty. Chapter 11 focuses on moms who are past the newborn stage, from the time their baby is six weeks to six months. And, finally, chapter 12 provides all the information that you need to help with your baby's sleep.

Reminders

- Sleep issues are almost universal for pregnant women and new moms.
- The most common sleep problems experienced include insomnia, not getting a good night's sleep, and feeling sleepy during the day.
- The average adult needs between 7 and 9 hours of sleep.
- Not getting enough sleep is going to affect your mood, cognitive ability, performance, health, and life satisfaction—basically, every aspect of your life.
- There are many things that you can do to help you no longer feel as sleep deprived, from the moment that you conceive through the first six months after your baby is born.

TWO

How We Sleep: The Basics

"Why do I always feel sleepy now that I'm pregnant?"
—*Melissa, 9 weeks pregnant*

"I worry that my baby is not getting restful sleep. He's always squirming and twitching when he's asleep."
—*Lauren, mom to 11-week-old Shaidan*

How much do you know about sleep? It's something that we all have spent over one-third of our lives doing (that's about 2,900 hours in the last year alone), but most of us have no idea what actually happens to our bodies while we sleep. To help you get a good night's sleep and no longer feel sleep deprived, it is important to have an understanding of sleep itself and how much sleep you actually need.

What Is Sleep?

SLEEP IS A very active time for our bodies. Surprisingly, sleep is not actually the "opposite" of being awake, as many people believe. Our brains and our bodies are quite busy when we sleep. For example, during REM sleep (see "Sleep Stages" below for a complete explanation) our brains are as active as when we are awake.

Sleep is a biological process, but one that is affected by what we do and what we think. If you worry all day about being able to fall asleep at bedtime, you will be so wired by the time you turn out the lights that it will be impossible to fall asleep. Drink a six-pack of Mountain Dew before bed and you'll be wide-eyed and bushy-tailed all night. This is something that adults rarely do, but teens do this all the time. Keep waking up all night to check the clock to see if it's the time that your baby usually gets up for a feeding and you'll have a hard time sleeping.

Our environment also affects sleep. For example, consider trying to sleep in a noisy hotel room—it can be impossible to sleep, even if you normally have no problems sleeping at home. When you're pregnant, you may find that you need to lower the temperature in your house or sleep with fewer blankets, as you're much more likely to get too hot during the night.

Sleep Stages

SLEEP IS NOT actually just one state. We don't just shut our eyes, fall asleep, and wake up later. Sleep is actually two separate states: (1) non-REM sleep, and (2) REM sleep. REM stands for "rapid eye movement" (your eyes move around under your lids as you sleep). Each of these two sleeping states and wake, which is our third state of being, involve different parts of the brain and brain chemicals (known as neurotransmitters).

During REM sleep and non-REM sleep, we are clearly asleep and are not responding to the world around us, quite different from when we are awake. At the same time, REM sleep and non-REM sleep are as different from one another as the difference between "awake" and "asleep."

Sleep itself is comprised of several sleep stages, which experts refer to as "sleep architecture." Each sleep stage is unique in its pattern of brain waves (electroencephalogram, or EEG) and body movements, particularly eye movements. The sleep stages also differ in the level of awareness of the sleeper and how easy (or difficult) it is to awaken her.

Non-REM Sleep

Non-REM sleep occurs in four stages, each with its own distinctive features.

STAGE ONE. Stage one sleep occurs when you feel drowsy and start to fall asleep. It is basically the transition between awake and asleep. If the phone rings or something else wakes you, you may not even realize that you have been asleep and will often deny that you were sleeping. You are not lying; you will actually think that you were awake. Stage one lasts for the first thirty seconds to five minutes of sleep.

Sometimes during stage one a person will awaken with a sudden jerk, often referred to as a "sleep start." These are common and totally normal. In addition, some people experience short periods of feeling like they are paralyzed as they drift off to sleep. This feeling of paralysis is the result of a short burst of REM sleep occurring just as you are falling asleep. This is more likely to happen when you are sleep deprived.

STAGE TWO. Stage two sleep is actually the beginning of "real" sleep. During stage two sleep, your body moves into a deeper state of sleep. You can still be easily wakened, but you are clearly asleep. Stage two makes up the greatest portion of your sleep, about 50 percent of the time you are asleep.

STAGES THREE AND FOUR. Stages three and four are usually considered together and are often referred to as "deep sleep," "slow-wave sleep," or "delta sleep." Your breathing and heart rate will be very regular and slow during deep sleep. For some people, sweating is common during these stages of sleep. It is also very difficult to be awakened from deep sleep. You may not hear a phone ringing or someone calling your name. When people sleep through earthquakes or major storms (or a crying baby!), it is because they are in deep sleep. If you do get awakened from deep sleep, you may be confused, and it will take you a few minutes to respond.

Stages three and four are the deepest stages of sleep and a time during which your body experiences the most positive and restorative effects of sleep. If you are not sleeping enough, you will spend more time in deep sleep to compensate. Following the first deep sleep period, of anywhere from a few minutes to an hour, there is a return to a lighter stage of sleep prior to the first REM period.

REM Sleep

In contrast, REM sleep is a very active type of sleep, and typically when you dream. Your eyes dart back and forth under your eyelids during this stage of sleep, hence the term rapid eye movement. Both your breathing and heart rate become irregular, although no sweating occurs. Other than the normal functioning of your organs, the majority of your body becomes paralyzed, and all of your muscles become extremely relaxed. Being essentially paralyzed during REM sleep is a good thing, as it protects you from acting out your dreams. Some people, though, experience minor twitching of their hands, legs, or face during REM sleep. (This is sometimes very obvious; you can observe it by watching your dog or cat during REM sleep.) And men usually get erections during REM sleep, which is why they typically wake with an erection (although that is obviously not an issue for you!). REM sleep accounts for 20 to 25 percent of a typical night's sleep.

Sleep Cycles

Sleep also has a very typical structure in terms of timing (cycles) of the sleep stages throughout the night. Non-REM and REM sleep periods alternate about every 90 minutes in adults. That is, your first 90 minutes asleep is all non-REM. After 90 minutes, a period of REM sleep will occur, followed by a return to non-REM sleep. After that, about every 90 minutes a REM period will occur.

The first REM periods of the night are quite short, lasting just a few minutes. As the night goes on, REM periods increase in length. Most REM sleep occurs in the last third of the night, and by early morning, much of your sleep is REM. This is the reason you are likely to be dreaming (or having a nightmare) when you awaken in the morning.

If you are sleep deprived, the first REM period will be earlier in the night, after only 30 or 40 minutes, and more REM sleep will occur. So your dreams may be much more vivid the first night that you get a good night's sleep after a period of being sleep deprived. People who are sleep deprived will also have more stages three and four sleep on nights they are catching up on their sleep.

Sleep, however, is not totally logical and one stage of sleep does not always follow the next. Although in general your body will cycle through all the stages of sleep, you may also move from one stage to another in no particular order. Some nights you may never have any stage three or four sleep. Other nights you will have a great deal.

There are several other things to know about sleep cycles. Most sleep cycles end in a short period of awakening from sleep, or a partial awakening called an "arousal," before you go on to the next sleep cycle. You can usually see it in someone else, as that person may shift positions or roll over at that point. You may also wake up completely. This is why you may wake up around the same time every single night, especially if you usually go to bed at the same time—you hit the end of a sleep cycle around the same time every night. Luckily, most of the time these brief arousals are followed by a rapid return to sleep, until the end of the next sleep cycle. You will likely be totally unaware of these brief arousals. These transitions can occur 4 to 5 times every night.

Changes in Sleep Architecture During Pregnancy

The studies are still trying to sort it out, but it does seem that sleep changes during pregnancy. Each trimester is characterized by different changes. Primarily, REM sleep tends to increase throughout pregnancy but interestingly reaches a peak during the thirty-third to thirty-sixth week, and decreases in the 3 to 4 weeks before delivery. Studies also seem to indicate that there is some reduction in deep sleep (stages three and four of non-REM sleep) during the third trimester. A decrease in these stages of sleep means that you feel less rested when you wake up in the morning.

Other changes also occur that make you feel sleepier when you are pregnant. Progesterone, a hormone that increases in your body when you are pregnant, makes women feel sleepy. In addition, your body is working overtime now that it is working for two. So you will need more sleep now than before you were pregnant.

Sleep Structure in Babies

NEWBORN BABIES SLEEP quite differently from adults. Infant sleep patterns actually begin to develop in the uterus, before birth. A developing baby of six or seven months' gestation experiences REM sleep, with non-REM sleep beginning shortly afterward. By the end of the eighth month, your baby's sleep patterns are well established.

Sleep researchers classify sleep stages in newborns as *active* sleep (REM) and *quiet* sleep (non-REM). During active sleep, infants are quite mobile. They may move their arms or legs, cry or whimper, and their eyes may be partly open. Their breathing is irregular, and their eyes may dart back and forth under their eyelids. During quiet sleep, infants are behaviorally, well, quiet. Their breathing is regular, and they lie very still. They may, however, have an occasional startle response or make sucking movements with their mouths. It is not until about six months that babies develop the four distinct stages of non-REM sleep.

Infants' active sleep (REM sleep) accounts for 50 percent of sleep, rather than the typical 20 to 25 percent in adults. In addition, their sleep cycle is closer to 50 to 60 minutes. This is why they wake up more often during the night!

And, finally, thanks to active REM sleep, your baby may not be as quiet during the night as you would expect. Many babies sigh in their sleep. Babies will smile, sigh, squeak, coo, moan, groan, and whimper in their sleep. It is all perfectly normal. Don't worry that your baby is not getting good solid sleep if he seems to be active during sleep.

Why Do We Sleep?

HERE'S A SURPRISING thing: after all these studies, researchers still have no definite idea of why we sleep. Every single animal sleeps, some for more time (the giant armadillo spends a huge amount of time asleep, at a whopping 18.1 hours) and some for less (the giraffe spends the least amount of time asleep, at just 1.9 hours a day).

There are many theories on the function of sleep. Some scientists believe that sleep is critical to our memory, in that information is sorted through, processed, and stored during sleep. Others view sleep as a restorative process in that sleep is rejuvenating. And even others believe that sleep developed as a protective mechanism, ensuring that we are not roaming about during the dangerous hours of the night. None of these theories, though, seems to completely and satisfactorily explain why we sleep.

Of course, rather than knowing why we sleep, we really only know what happens to us if we don't. We know that sleep deprivation affects just about every aspect of our functioning Basically, sleep is critical to our staying alert, to our optimum brain function, and to our survival.

What Controls Sleep

We are just beginning to have a true understanding of the very complicated biological processes that determine when we are awake and when we are asleep. The systems that control sleep have their origins in the brain and involve neurotransmitters (chemical messengers). But the regulation of sleep is also influenced by many other factors, including all of the many things that compete with sleep for our time.

The two major systems involved in the control of sleep are called the *sleep drive* and the *sleep* or *circadian clock*. Both of these systems are acting at the same time. Sometimes they are working together (in the same direction) and sometimes they are in opposition to each other. How sleepy or awake you are at any given time is the result of the combined forces of the sleep drive and the sleep clock.

SLEEP DRIVE. As you likely imagine, how much you feel alert or sleepy is dependent upon how long you have been awake and how much sleep (and the quality of that sleep) you got the night before. This is known as the sleep drive. Your sleep drive starts out at a very low level when you wake up in the morning and then builds steadily over the course of the day (unless you take a nap), with the drive or "pressure" to sleep becoming stronger the longer you are up. Once you've gotten a good night's sleep, the sleep drive returns to a very low level.

SLEEP CLOCK. The sleep clock, otherwise known as the circadian clock, on the other hand, is a regular internal rhythm of sleep and wake that is controlled by a specific area of the brain (its actual name is the *suprachiasmatic nucleus*). There are two points in the 24-hour day when you are at your sleepiest and two points when you are at your most alert and awake. The periods of peak sleepiness occur in the late afternoon between 3:00 and 5:00 p.m. and in the middle of the night between 3:00 and 5:00 a.m. (as you would expect). The two periods of peak alertness happen in the early to mid-morning and in mid- to late evening. This is why you may feel that you get a second wind in the early evening.

Your sleep clock is also affected by cues in the environment that help keep it on a 24-hour time course. The most influential environmental cue is light. Light influences the circadian clock by suppressing the body's production of the hormone melatonin. Melatonin, which is normally at its peak in the evening and at its lowest point in the morning, is one of the body's most powerful sleep messengers. So exposure to light in the evening slows the body's production of melatonin and makes it more difficult to fall asleep. This is why it's best to keep lights dim at night, especially as you are getting ready for bed. Light exposure in the morning has the helpful effect of suppressing melatonin and waking you up. So it's very helpful to eat breakfast in a sunny part of the house, go for a morning walk, and not to wear sunglasses when driving to work or dropping off your kids at day care. Other cues that affect the sleep clock are the timing of daily activities. Having routines such as eating meals at the same time every day will actually help you sleep better at night.

Can You Make Up for Lost Sleep by Sleeping In the Next Day?

Deb is the mother of 5-month-old twins. During the week Deb goes to bed between 11:00 p.m. and midnight and has to get up for work at 6:00 a.m. Usually the twins wake her at least once or twice during the night. On weekends, her husband takes over and she is able to sleep in and get eight or nine hours of sleep. However, she still feels tired.

Deb is finding that it is not easy to make up for lost sleep. Some studies show that it may take up to three weeks to make up for lost sleep. This means that sleeping in on weekends will not solve the problem of not getting enough sleep during the week, nor will a one- or two-week vacation when you can sleep in each day. If you are pregnant, you may be able to take a three-week vacation, but it's doubtful if you have a baby that you could sleep in that much.

Sleep is not like a bank account, though, where you need to literally make up for all the hours that you missed over the past week, month, or year. How you feel is more a function of how you slept last night and over the past week or two. So try to get as much sleep as you can every night so that you don't end up in the situation where it's going to take you a long time to catch up on hours of missed sleep.

"Why Do I Feel So Tired During the Day?"

Samantha was 9 weeks pregnant. She couldn't understand why she was having problems sleeping. She fell asleep at bedtime with no problem but woke up several times during the night. Most of the time she was able to fall back to sleep right away, but there were nights when she was awake for an hour or two. Every morning she had to drag herself out of bed to get ready for work.

SLEEP PROBLEMS ARE incredibly common, especially during pregnancy and after the baby is born. According to the National Sleep Foundation's *Sleep in America Poll 2007*, 84 percent of both pregnant women and new moms (women with a baby younger than 6 months) report sleep problems at least a few nights a week. This is in comparison to 67 percent of women in general.

There are many different reasons for feeling sleepy during the day. Below are just a few:

- **NOT GETTING ENOUGH SLEEP AT NIGHT.** This one sounds obvious, but the most common reason that women feel sleepy during the day is the simple fact that they don't get enough sleep at night. The typical adult woman needs between 7 and 9 hours of sleep every night. You may actually need even more than this, especially when you are pregnant. Surprisingly, not only will not getting enough sleep make you feel tired during the day, but it can actually make it harder for you to sleep at night. You may find that you wake more often, are more restless, and have vivid dreams that can disrupt your sleep.

- **POOR QUALITY SLEEP.** Although you may be in bed and asleep for your required 7 to 9 hours, the quality of your sleep may not be high quality. For example, if you are uncomfortable or restless, you'll wake up in the morning not feeing like you got a good night's sleep. Snoring and sleep apnea can disturb your sleep, waking you up numerous times during the night (even as many as 50 or 60 times an hour!). You will likely not even be aware of these very brief awakenings, but you'll definitely notice it in the morning when you feel just as tired as when you went to bed.

- **ENVIRONMENT.** Everything that surrounds you during the night when you sleep can have a major impact, anything from basic things, such as the temperature of your bedroom and the comfort of your bed, to other environmental factors, such as being awakened by your child or your snoring husband. Street noise can disrupt your sleep, as can having your cat or dog sleep with you in your bed. There was even a study that showed that sleep problems are more common in pet owners who let their pets sleep with them.

- **HORMONES.** Especially during pregnancy, and even in the first month or two after your baby is born, hormones can play a big part in how well you sleep and how sleepy you feel during the day. Progesterone, a hormone that is produced in large quantities while you are pregnant, can both make you feel sleepy during the day and disrupt your sleep at night.

- **MEDICAL OR MENTAL HEALTH ISSUES.** If you have any medical problems, such as a thyroid imbalance, pain, or obesity, you are at risk for having a sleep problem. Mental health issues, such as depression and anxiety, can also interfere with sleep. Be sure to discuss any medical or mental health issues with your doctor as they pertain to how well you sleep at night. As you might imagine, how well you sleep at night will affect how you feel during the day, and vice versa. The relationship between sleep and these two areas goes in both directions.

Often there is more than one reason for sleep problems. You may be experiencing restless legs syndrome, being awakened by your baby, and your husband's snoring all at the same time. No wonder you're not getting a good night's sleep!

Do You Have a Sleep Problem?

SLEEP PROBLEMS FALL into two major groups: (1) those that make it hard for you to fall asleep and stay asleep, and (2) those that interfere with the quality of your sleep. Some sleep problems are immediately obvious in that you can't fall asleep or you wake up during the night. Other sleep problems are not so obvious, such as sleep apnea (see chapter 9) and periodic limb movement disorder (see chapter 8). Many times the only symptom is feeling terrible the next day, as if you didn't get a good night's sleep the night before. Sleep problems, though, can have a significant impact on your health and functioning, so it's best to recognize the symptoms of a possible sleep problem.

Quiz

Pittsburg Sleep Quality Index Scale

THE PITTSBURG SLEEP Quality Index is a standard questionnaire that is used in sleep clinics and sleep studies to assess sleep quality.

INSTRUCTIONS: The following questions relate to your usual sleep habits during the past month only. Your answers should indicate the most accurate reply for the majority of days and nights in the past month. Please answer all questions.

During the past month, how often have you had trouble sleeping because you ...	Not during the past month	Less than once a week	Once or twice a week	Three or more times a week
Cannot get to sleep within 30 minutes	0	1	2	3
Wake up in the middle of the night or early morning	0	1	2	3
Have to get up to use the bathroom	0	1	2	3
Cannot breathe comfortably	0	1	2	3
Cough or snore loudly	0	1	2	3
Feel too cold	0	1	2	3

During the past month, how often have you had trouble sleeping because you . . .	Not during the past month	Less than once a week	Once or twice a week	Three or more times a week
Feel too hot	0	1	2	3
Have bad dreams	0	1	2	3
Have pain	0	1	2	3
Other reason(s)	0	1	2	3
During the past month, how often have you taken medicine (prescribed or over the counter) to help you sleep?	0	1	2	3
During the past month, how often have you had trouble staying awake while driving, eating meals, or engaging in social activity?	0	1	2	3
During the past month, how much of a problem has it been for you to keep up enthusiasm to get things done?	0	1	2	3

	Very good	Fairly good	Fairly bad	Very bad
During the past month, how would you rate your sleep quality overall?	0	1	2	3

SCORING: A score between 0 and 5 indicates that you are a good sleeper. If, however, your score is 6 or greater, this is an indication of poor quality sleep.

Reminders

- Sleep is comprised of two major states, non-REM and REM sleep.
- Sleep is controlled by two systems, sleep drive and the circadian clock. Sleep drive is based on how long you have been awake and how well you slept the night before. The circadian clock is our regular internal rhythm of wake and sleep.
- Feeling sleepy during the day can be the result of not getting enough sleep at night, poor quality sleep, and hormones.
- Sleep problems fall into two groups: those that make it hard to fall asleep and stay asleep, and those that interfere with the quality of your sleep.

THREE

Tips for Improving Your Sleep

"All night long I toss and turn for hours trying to fall asleep.
I just can't get comfortable, especially as I've always slept
on my stomach."

—*Lisa, 19 weeks pregnant with her second baby*

"I usually drink several cups of coffee during the day to
stay awake and give me energy, but then I feel jittery at
bedtime. I'm worried that if I don't drink the coffee I will
fall asleep while driving, especially when I'm driving home
from work."

—*Marie, mom to 4-month-old Sophie*

Believe it or not, there is actually a term
called "sleep hygiene." Just the way dental hygiene means taking
care of your teeth, sleep hygiene refers to developing good sleep
habits. We usually don't think about creating habits and routines to sleep well, but it really makes a difference. Proper sleep
hygiene includes maintaining a consistent sleep schedule, having
a proper bedtime routine, and avoiding certain activities close
to bedtime. These general suggestions are even more important
now that you are pregnant or a new mom.

Provided in this chapter are a number of simple methods you
can use to improve the way you sleep. You'll see that the list of
ideas is long! Try to stick with as many as you can to help you
sleep well at night and feel your best during the day.

. . .

Put Yourself on a "Sleep Hygiene" Routine

ONE OF THE biggest impediments to sleep is living in our 24/7 society. You can accomplish just about anything in the middle of the night that you can during the day. You can go grocery shopping, purchase airline tickets, or order clothes from a catalog as easily at 1:00 in the morning as you can at 1:00 in the afternoon. Not only does this mean that you are up in the middle of the night, but it also means that others are awake all night—the cashier at the grocery store and the sales clerk answering the telephone for the catalog company.

Even though you can get things done day or night, try to stick with a traditional schedule of activities during the day and sleeping at night. Do not get lured into doing things in the middle of the night just because you can or just because it may be easier.

Maintain a Regular Daily Schedule of Activities

Try to keep a set schedule during the day. Eat meals at the same times and plan your activities to fit a similar schedule. You may need to change your schedule from your prepregnancy days, but sticking to a schedule will help tremendously. While you are pregnant, having more frequent meals or snacks scheduled throughout the day will help you feel better. As a mom, make sure that you remember to eat breakfast and lunch. Build into each day a few minutes to read the newspaper or catch up on your favorite news program. Make sure that you take time to take a shower and get dressed!

Keep a Sleep Schedule

Try to go to bed at the same time every night and wake up at the same time every morning. This will help set your body's inner clock. Your body produces a hormone called melatonin, which governs your sleep-wake cycle. If you go to bed at the same time every night, your melatonin will consistently peak at that time, which will help you fall asleep right on cue. Be sure to also stick to the same schedule on weekends as well as weekdays. Many women end up staying up much later on weekends and sleeping in later in the morning. But if you shift too much, your body will have a hard time getting back on your weekday schedule. So it is best to go to bed within an hour of your usual bedtime every night of the week.

Should You Take a Nap?

NAPS ARE ESPECIALLY common for pregnant women and new moms. A little more than half of all pregnant women and 40 percent of new moms take a nap at least twice a week, compared to 30 percent of all women.

Naps can be wonderful but they can cause problems. On the positive side, short naps of 30 to 45 minutes can improve alertness, take the edge off sleepiness, and decrease fatigue. But if you are having problems sleeping, avoid napping, as this can interfere with nighttime sleep. Some women find that when they take a nap in the afternoon, especially if it's too late in the afternoon or too long a nap, then it's hard to fall asleep at bedtime.

Develop a Bedtime Routine

Every night Lena does the same things at bedtime. She picks out her clothes for the next day, changes into her pajamas, and sets her alarm clock. She then washes up and brushes her teeth. Once she is ready for bed, she reads for at least 20 minutes, tuning out the world. Right before she turns out the light, she slathers herself with her favorite scented lotion, which she saves as a special treat just for bedtime.

Bedtime routines are as important for adults as they are for babies. And they are especially important when you are a new mom, as this may be one of the only times of the day that you focus on yourself. Bedtime routines let your body know it is time to sleep before you even get into bed, which will make it easier to fall asleep. Your bedtime routine should include three or four activities that are the same every night (just like a baby's bedtime routine). At the beginning of your routine, set your alarm clock and figure out your plan for the next day. Many women do those two things last, immediately before climbing into bed. However, thinking about all the things that you need to do the next day may rev you up and make you anxious. Instead, do those things first and then do something relaxing to help you wind down.

Include a relaxing activity in your bedtime routine, whether that is writing in your journal, listening to some music, applying your favorite lotion, or reading a book. Taking a warm bath or shower can also help you relax after a busy day and help make you feel sleepy. Bedtime is not the time to try and slog through a book that is allegedly "good for you." Go for the guilty-pleasure novel and lose yourself in another world. Again, you also don't want to do anything immediately before bed that is too alerting, such as paying bills, watching a scary movie (or even the nightly news), or having an intense discussion.

A Sleep-Friendly Lifestyle

A ROUTINE IS just one aspect of good sleep hygiene. Some things that you do right at bedtime, such as drinking too many liquids, as well as other things that you may be doing during the day will affect how well you sleep at night. Drink a double espresso in the late afternoon and expect to later be lying in bed wide awake. Same thing with smoking during the day or not exercising. All are going to lead to less sleep and feeling sleep deprived.

Manage Your Fluids

Be sure to drink lots of fluids during the day. Some say that adults need to drink eight 8-ounce glasses every day, but check with your doctor about what you should personally drink. Cut down on your fluid intake before bedtime, though, to reduce multiple trips to the bathroom during the night. This is true whether you are pregnant or nursing.

Eat a Light Snack

Eating a light snack prior to bedtime can stave off hunger and help ease nausea. Going to bed hungry can interrupt your sleep, and if you are having morning sickness (or in this case nighttime sickness), eating a snack can help a great deal. In addition, a cup of hot tea (decaffeinated, of course) or warm milk can help make you drowsy.

Prevent heartburn by not eating large amounts of spicy, acidic, or fried foods, especially close to bedtime. Even eating these foods at dinnertime can still cause you problems hours later when you head to bed. Also, avoid dairy foods if they upset your stomach.

> ### Sleep-Inducing Snacks
>
> **THERE IS ACTUALLY** nothing that will literally induce sleep, but there are some foods that are better to have as a snack at bedtime than others. Snacks that are low in sugar, high in protein, and include complex carbohydrates are best. Eat some oatmeal raisin cookies, a peanut butter sandwich, or a granola bar. These are much better choices than junk food or sweets.

Avoid Caffeine

Most experts agree that drinking small amounts of caffeine (equal to one or two 8-ounce cups of coffee) during pregnancy is safe. However, avoid caffeinated beverages, foods, and medications in the late afternoon and evening. Some women find that they are so sensitive to caffeine that they have to avoid it by lunchtime so that they can sleep at night. Note that many sodas, including Mountain Dew and some orange sodas, contain caffeine (see pages 42–43 for a list of caffeinated items). For example, Sunkist Orange has 42 milligrams of caffeine per 12 ounces, whereas Diet Sunkist Orange has none. Check the ingredients listing on the label. Even chocolate and other foods with caffeine in them, such as coffee yogurt or coffee ice cream, can keep you up at night. For those with restless legs syndrome or periodic limb movements in sleep (see chapter 8), caffeine will make both of these conditions worse.

How Much Caffeine Are You Consuming?

CAFFEINE CAN RESULT in difficulties falling asleep and staying asleep.

Product	Serving Size	Caffeine Content (mg)
SODA		
Coca-Cola	8 oz	23
Diet Coke	8 oz	31
Pepsi	8 oz	25
Diet Pepsi	8 oz	24
Dr Pepper/Diet Dr Pepper	8 oz	28
Mountain Dew/Diet Mountain Dew	8 oz	37
Sunkist Orange soda	8 oz	28
Tab	8 oz	47
Red Bull	330 mL	80
COFFEE/TEA		
Cappuccino	6 oz	35
Coffee, decaf	8 oz	5
Starbucks coffee, tall	8 oz	250
Starbucks coffee, grande	12 oz	375
Starbucks coffee, venti	16 oz	550
Iced tea	8 oz	25
Snapple iced tea (all kinds)	8 oz	21
FOOD ITEMS		
Baker's chocolate	1 oz	26
Chocolate milk	8 oz	5

Dark chocolate, semisweet	1 oz	20
Coffee ice cream	8 oz	58
OVER-THE-COUNTER MEDICATIONS		
Dexatrim	1 tablet	200
Excedrin, max. strength	2 tablets	130
NoDoz, max. strength; Vivarin	1 tablet	200
NoDoz, regular strength	1 tablet	100

Avoid Alcohol

Hopefully, you are avoiding alcohol while you are pregnant and nursing, but here's another reason to skip that evening drink. Alcoholic beverages interfere with sleep. They may help you to fall asleep more quickly, but they usually lead to your waking in the middle of the night.

Quit Smoking

Smoking harms not only yourself but everyone else in your family. It can harm your developing baby and the lungs of your children. Studies have shown that smoking also increases the risk of your baby dying from sudden infant death syndrome (SIDS). And smoking will make it more difficult for you to get a good night's sleep.

· · ·

Exercise

Exercise can help you sleep better. It is also great for both your mental and physical health. Exercise will keep you healthy, improve your circulation, and even reduce leg cramps.

The best time to exercise to help you sleep well is in the late afternoon or early evening, about five to six hours before bed-time. Avoid exercising within four hours of bedtime, as it may wake you up too much. It will also raise your internal body temperature. You actually want to lower your body tempera-ture at bedtime, as that will help you fall asleep.

Talk to your doctor to help you develop an exercise plan that will be safe while you are pregnant and one that you can start after the birth of your baby. Discuss how much exercise you should be getting, as well as different types of exercise that may be best for you.

Stop Worrying

Having a baby is a big responsibility and a huge lifestyle change, so it's natural to feel anxious. I certainly know that to stop worrying is much easier said than done! But constant worry will definitely keep you up at night and cause more stress during the day. Figure out what works best for you when it comes to calming your nerves. For example, some women keep a worry list on a notepad by their bed, writing down all their questions, concerns, and things that they need to do so that they can stop thinking about them before they go to sleep. On the other hand, some women find that having their worry list next to them at night makes it feel as if they can't get away from their worries.

Others find that setting a "worry time" during the day works. Take 30 minutes at some point of the day to worry. If you start to worry at other times of the day, stop and remind yourself that you are only allowed to worry during your designated worry time. It may sound silly but it really works.

Make Your Bedroom a Sleep Haven

To ensure that you get a good night's sleep, turn your bedroom into a calm, relaxing environment. Avoid doing other activities in bed other than sleep (and sex, of course). If your bedroom is a mess with clutter everywhere and a desk strewn with paperwork, it's no surprise that you have a hard time sleeping. Making your bedroom a true haven from the outside world will help you sleep better at night and will make your bedroom a place where you want to be. This will lead to your spending more time there, resulting in your getting more sleep!

What makes a bedroom peaceful? The answer is different for everyone, so flip through some home design books of wonderful bedrooms to see what appeals to your sense of calm. Once you find a few pictures that strike a chord with you, study what about these designer rooms pulls at you. Is it the wonderfully large bed with fluffy pillows? Is it the soothing color of the walls? Is it the corner chair that looks like it would be glorious to cuddle up in and read a good book?

Your Bed

Next, evaluate your bed. Make sure that your bed is comfortable. Many manufacturers recommend replacing your mattress and box spring every 8 to 10 years. You're the best judge, though, of whether your bed needs replacing. Also think about your bedding, including your mattress pad. Some women find sleeping on a down mattress cover to be heavenly, whereas others prefer a firmer sleeping surface. Consider your blankets. Do you prefer a lightweight blanket or a heavier comforter? Does a duvet feel heavenly or as if it's smothering you? And finally, think about your pillow. Is it past its prime? Do you prefer feather or foam? Most stomach sleepers do best with a soft pillow, whereas back sleepers find firm pillows most comfortable.

Kate couldn't believe it. She had been having so many problems sleeping over the past month. It was wintertime and it was cold at night, so she was using flannel sheets. One day she made the bed with regular cotton sheets, since all of her flannel sheets were in the laundry. She was stunned. That night, she slept better than ever. She realized that the flannel sheets made it much harder for her to roll over in bed, and all of her extra pillows got tangled in the sheets.

Amazingly, it may be something as simple as your bedding that is causing you sleep problems at night. Try different combinations of sheets, blankets, comforters, and pillows. See what combination helps you sleep best. Replace sheets that are pilling or that feel scratchy. You may be quite surprised by what a difference such a small change can make in how well you sleep at night, and thus feel during the day.

Pregnancy Pillows

THERE ARE MANY types of pregnancy (maternity) pillows available. They come in all shapes and sizes. Some are shaped as huge U's, some are long and wrap around your entire body, and others cradle your body. You may want to check them out and see if any of them look like they'll be helpful.

Make Your Bedroom Sleep-Friendly

Finally, be sure your bedroom is quiet, cool, and dark at night. Run a fan or a white-noise machine to drown out sounds from the outdoors (this is not always best if it drowns out the sound of your baby if she needs you, although dampening the normal sounds your baby makes while sleeping can be helpful). It may be worth investing in room-darkening shades or blinds if your bedroom is too light. Some curtains and shades will also absorb sound, as will carpeting. Finally, keep pets out of the bedroom, as they are notorious for jumping onto the bed and waking a person up (there was even a study published on the disruption of sleep by pets).

Get Electronics Out of Your Bedroom

Dana and Tim were used to living in a one-bedroom apartment where their bedroom doubled as their workspace. When they finally moved into a house, they made the same choice, putting their computer table in the alcove of their bedroom. Dana continued the bad habit of checking her e-mail right before turning out the lights at night.

Electronics are beginning to dominate the bedroom. Check out any decorating magazine that depicts perfect bedrooms. There is not a television, computer, or cell phone in sight. Now look around your own bedroom. It's likely a sea of electronics, all plugged in and keeping you wired at bedtime and throughout the night. Electronics belong elsewhere in your home. They should not be overtaking your bedroom.

Turning off the world will help you get a better night's sleep. You will be amazed at how much better you feel during the day if you unplug yourself at night. This means turning off the television, the computer, instant messaging, cell phones, and PDAs (BlackBerries and PalmPilots). Even better is to declare your bedroom an electronics-free zone and not let any of these things enter.

Wear Comfy Sleeping Attire

Wear loose-fitting, comfortable sleeping attire. Sexy lingerie may look great, but it won't help you sleep. The more comfortable you are, the better you will sleep. Cotton and other natural fibers will be the most comfortable. Synthetics trap moisture and can leave you feeling damp and chilly during the night. If your feet get cold, wear socks. You will be surprised at what a difference a pair of socks can make in keeping your whole body warm.

Some women find that sleeping in the nude is actually the most comfortable. Another choice is just to wear underwear and nothing else. Or wear a nightshirt and nothing underneath. You need to figure out what is the most comfortable for you.

Maternity and Mom-Friendly Sleepwear

PAJAMAS. Now that you're pregnant, you may want to think a bit more about what you wear at night. Those sexy lingerie nightgowns may not be the thing to be wearing right now. Instead, flannel pajamas may become your best friend. A favorite pair of sweats and your husband's old T-shirt may be your choice for perfect nighttime wear.

SLEEPING BRA. In addition, many women find that a sleep bra makes them more comfortable, especially during the third trimester. Adding some nighttime support during pregnancy can be helpful, especially if your breasts are sore or become uncomfortable.

MOMS. Moms need to think about what they wear at night, too. If you are nursing, you are likely going to want to continue sleeping in either a sleeping bra or a nursing bra. Sleeping with nursing pads can also be helpful, especially if you are concerned about leaking during the night.

Sharing a Bed

Although Fiona and Tony had been married for three years, they still disagreed over how cold to keep their bedroom at night. They also often argued about what position to sleep in, as Tony was a cuddler and liked Fiona next to him when he was sleeping, whereas Fiona had a hard time sleeping with Tony touching her. They finally had to have a long talk about how to manage their different styles. They decided to buy an electric mattress pad that had dual controls so that Fiona could keep her side of the bed warm at night. In addition, they agreed to cuddle at night until Tony fell asleep. At that point, it was okay for Fiona to roll over to her side of the bed for the rest of the night.

If you share a bed with your husband or partner, you will not be surprised to hear that this can disrupt your sleep. There are many reasons, from hogging the covers, to snoring so loudly at night that you are sure there is a buzzsaw nearby, to demanding that the television stay on all night.

Negotiation is the key to your sleeping better when sharing a bed. Come up with solutions that work for both of you. As a first step, communicate with your partner. Discuss what helps both of you get a good night's sleep and then work together to achieve these goals.

- **NOT ENOUGH ROOM.** If you find that one of you is always feeling pushed off the side of the bed or there just isn't enough room for the two of you, splurging on a king-size bed can make a world of difference. Don't even think of it as "splurging," but rather as a necessity so that you can both get the sleep that you need.

- **TOO MUCH NOISE.** If your bed partner makes too much noise during the night, especially if he comes to bed later than you or gets up earlier, try running a fan or white-noise machine. The constant hum can help drown out the noise of the opening and closing of doors and dresser drawers. And if you can get used to them, earplugs can be a very helpful way to reduce jarring noise.

- **TOO HOT OR TOO COLD.** Wanting different temperatures in your bedroom at night is one of the most common complaints made by couples. Rather than arguing over the temperature of the room, try adding extra blankets to the side of the bed of the person who is too cold at night. For example, if you have a king-size bed, make the bed with a king-size blanket. Then add a twin-size blanket to just one side of the bed. This will keep you sleeping together, but one of you can stay cool and the other warm throughout the night. There are also heated mattress pads and heated blankets with dual controls so you can warm just one side of the bed.

- **HOGGING THE COVERS.** Your partner may not even realize it, but he may be stealing the covers throughout the night. Avoid the tug-of-war. Get a blanket or comforter that is bigger than your bed. So if you have a queen-size bed, buy a king-size comforter. There will be plenty of covers for the two of you.

Sharing a Bed or a Room with Your Baby

YOU ARE GOING to have to decide whether you want to share your room with your baby. Some women find that having their baby sleep in their room helps them sleep at night, as they don't have to head to another room if the baby wakes up. On the other hand, you may not sleep as well if you hear your baby's every squeak and squeal. Read more about sharing a room and/or your bed with your baby in chapter 12.

- **LOUD SNORING.** If your bed partner is snoring, the best thing that you can do is get him to talk to his doctor about it or see a sleep specialist. Most snoring can be treated! In lieu of getting professional help, some people find that making some changes will decrease their snoring. Cutting out alcohol in the evening can make a big difference. Losing a few pounds can, too. Some people find that just a five-pound difference in their weight will make the snoring go away. Others find that sleeping on their backs is the only time they snore. In this case, have him put on a pocketed T-shirt backward and put a tennis ball in the pocket (now on his back). This technique will keep him off his back. Worst-case scenario—get some earplugs for yourself!

- **NEEDS A FAN TO SLEEP.** Many people sleep with a fan on in their room to fall asleep. If you can't stand the fan being on, figure out why your bed partner finds it helpful. If it's the air blowing on him, then try putting the fan closer to his side of the bed. If it's the noise of the fan, try switching to a white-noise machine.

- **DIFFERENT SLEEP SCHEDULES.** Night owls seem to marry early birds. You may find that you and your partner are on two totally different clocks, with one of you revving up just when the other is ready to head to bed and the other raring to go first thing in the morning when you can barely mumble a coherent sentence before 9:00 in the morning. First of all, accept your differences and work around them. Let the night owl stay up later. If bedtime is your time for intimacy, the night owl can get back up and stay up later while the early bird drifts off to sleep. Set separate alarm clocks to allow you to get up at different times of the night. A nightlight in your room can help. This way, the night owl can find his (or her) way to bed without disturbing the other, and the early bird can get dressed in the morning without turning on overhead lights.

- **JUST CAN'T TAKE IT.** And finally, if you share a bed with someone who is a snorer, a kicker, or a cover-stealer, you may want to sleep elsewhere, at least for the time being.

Get Fluffy and Fido Out of Your Bed

THE NATIONAL SLEEP Foundation's *Sleep in America Poll 2007* found that 17 percent of women report that pets interfere with their sleep at night. This was in contrast to 20 percent of women of all ages reporting that taking care of children interrupted their sleep. Thus, pets were a very close second to kids in interrupting sleep. Pets are much more likely to disrupt your sleep if they are in your bed. So it may well be worth getting Fluffy and Fido in their own beds, so you can get the sleep you need.

Juggling Sleep with Shift Work

Lindsay worked the night shift as a police dispatcher. On most nights, she worked from 11:00 P.M. to 7:00 A.M., although there were some days that she was required to go in from 3:00 to 11:00 P.M. There were benefits to this schedule in that she and her husband didn't have to pay for any child care. She took care of their 5-month-old during the day and her husband took over at night. It wasn't ideal, though, as Lindsay was often exhausted, and it was hard to find family time.

WOMEN WHO ARE shift workers have added challenges when it comes to sleep. Working night shifts or changing shifts can create havoc when it comes to getting adequate sleep, and it makes it hard to fall asleep. Our bodies were made to be awake during the day and asleep at night. Being a shift worker is totally contrary to our biological makeup. Working at night or on rotating shifts is also hard on families, as it takes away from family time. In addition, shift work interferes with other social and fun times, as shift workers are often working at times when others are heading out to have fun.

You can do a number of things to help manage your sleep while doing shift work that are less drastic than finding a new job:

- **GET ENOUGH SLEEP.** Most shift workers get less sleep than day workers. Make sleep a priority and schedule enough time for sleep.
- **GO TO SLEEP RIGHT AWAY.** It is best to head to bed right away when you get home from work.

- **NAP BEFORE HEADING TO WORK.** If you can't get your needed 7 to 9 hours of sleep, nap before heading to work. It's much better than skipping sleep.
- **CAFFEINE.** If you rely on caffeine to keep you awake and alert, it's better to have caffeine in the beginning or the middle of a shift. Caffeine too late in your shift will keep you awake when you finally get home.
- **EAT HEALTHILY AND EXERCISE.** Some of the negative effects of shift work are due to poor diet and lack of exercise. It is much harder to have a healthy breakfast or make a nutritious dinner when you are eating at opposite times from the rest of the world. Exercise can also be a challenge when you are working odd hours of the day and night. Try to exercise after you sleep rather than before heading to bed. Exercise is alerting and will raise your body temperature, making it harder to fall asleep.
- **MANAGE LIGHT.** If you work the night shift, head straight home at the end of your shift, avoid the sunlight, and sleep in a dark room. Wear sunglasses and install room-darkening shades. Light in the morning will wake you up and tell your body that it's time to be revving up for the day, not getting ready to head to bed. On the other hand, keep your workplace as bright as possible to help you keep you alert. There are even special lights that you can install to expose yourself to bright light during the evening or night.
- **IMPOSE A SLEEP-FRIENDLY ZONE.** Have friends and family members avoid calling you or visiting during times when you need to sleep. Turn off the ringer on the phone, just in case. Sleep in a faraway part of the house (if possible) if others in your home are up and

about during your sleep times. Ask family members to wear headphones when watching television or listening to music (not too hard in this age of iPods). Impose a ban on vacuuming and dishwashing when you are trying to sleep. And finally, schedule repairs and deliveries to occur after your sleep time.

- **MANAGING SHIFTS.** If your shift rotates, it's easier to adjust to a schedule that rotates from day shift to evening shift to night shift. This is much easier than adjusting to a shift that goes in reverse.

- **CONSIDER A BRIEF NAP DURING YOUR SHIFT.** If possible, take a 10- to 20-minute planned nap during your shift. It is better to plan for sleep than it is to fall asleep on the job.

- **STICK WITH THE SAME SCHEDULE ON WEEKENDS AND ON DAYS OFF.** As tempting as it may be to shift to regular waking hours on weekends and days off, it's best to keep your body clock on your usual workday schedule.

- **BALANCE WORK, FAMILY, AND SLEEP.** It can be quite difficult to balance all aspects of your life as a shift worker, as you are likely sleeping or working when everyone else is at home, such as during dinner or bedtime. Try to schedule special time with your family and your friends. If you work in the evening, call home at bedtime to share in the good-nights. Enjoy cuddle time with your kids in the morning when they are getting up for the day and you are heading for bed.

There are also things that you can do to feel more alert on the job, especially if you are not getting enough sleep. One caution is that you are most likely to hit your lowest period around 4:00 a.m., so be cautious at this time of the night.

- Take short breaks while at work.
- Talk with coworkers to help you stay awake and alert.
- Take a short nap of 10 to 20 minutes.
- Do some physical activity during your shift, whether that is walking around the block, climbing stairs, or just a few jumping jacks.
- Eat healthy snacks and schedule regular meals.

Reminders

- Put yourself on a routine, including going to bed at around the same time every day, waking up around the same time every morning, and creating a sleep-inducing bedtime routine
- Avoid caffeine, alcohol, and nicotine. All will interfere with getting a good night's sleep. They are also not good for you.
- Make your bedroom a sleep haven. This means creating a soothing atmosphere, having a comfortable bed, and getting all the electronics out of your bedroom.
- Figure out solutions to sleep differences so that you and your partner can share a bed and get a good night's sleep. Get pets out of your bed, too, if they are keeping you up at night.
- If you are a shift worker, you need to work extra hard to manage your schedule and get the sleep that you need.

PART II

Sleep and Pregnancy: Trimester by Trimester

FOUR

The First Trimester

> "All that I want to do is sleep, but I can't, as I have a
> 2-year-old and a 5-year-old. I would do anything
> to be able to take a nap."
> —*Sondra, 8 weeks pregnant*

> "I can't believe that I am this tired. I'm in bed by eight
> every night. I just can't keep my eyes open."
> —*Elizabeth, 11 weeks pregnant*

Congratulations! There is nothing more exhilarating than finding out that you are pregnant. Well, it can also be frightening, overwhelming, nerve-wracking, and all-around earth shattering—those feelings of entering unknown territory. If you have never been pregnant, there are many exciting surprises ahead. And if this is not your first pregnancy, you may be surprised at how each pregnancy is so different.

In addition to all the physical and psychological changes in your life, there will also be lots of emotional changes. You may be feeling great or you may be feeling lousy—and part of this has to do with how much sleep you're getting and how well you are sleeping. Interestingly, one study showed that pregnant women who have previously been pregnant get an extra 45 minutes sleep at night. It could be that these women understand from experience that they need to make sleep a priority. Get a bad night's sleep and you'll be dragging. Get a good night's sleep and you'll feel great. Getting that extra sleep will make your pregnancy a more positive experience and make you feel more energized throughout the day.

Most women think that sleep problems develop only in the second half of pregnancy, once a growing belly makes for a hard time finding a comfortable sleeping position. However, sleep problems often begin in the early days of the first trimester. Surging hormones, increasing needs to urinate throughout the night, and nausea all contribute to difficulties sleeping. Sleep can also be disrupted during the first trimester because of worries and concerns, whether that is fears of miscarriage, concerns about the impact of pregnancy and having a child on other aspects of your life, or deciding how to tell others about the pregnancy. Other issues that some pregnant women face in the early days of pregnancy include overwhelming daytime and evening fatigue and increased need for nighttime sleep.

This chapter will help you deal with all of these sleep issues and make sure that you get the sleep that you (and your developing brand-new baby) need. Dealing with this fatigue and sleepiness, a suggested sleep schedule, and ways to solve sleep problems are presented.

Common Causes of Sleep Problems During the First Trimester

As soon as Tricia got pregnant, she awoke frequently throughout the night. She had never had this problem before, as she had always been a sound sleeper, able to drift off to sleep anywhere—even on airplanes. She couldn't believe that she was already having problems sleeping at only 7 weeks pregnant.

THERE ARE SO many reasons that women have trouble sleeping during the first trimester of pregnancy. If it isn't one thing, it's another: you may feel nauseous, constantly need to run to the bathroom, or you could be having intense dreams. You may also develop a sleep problem, such as restless legs syndrome or snoring. These sleep issues can affect anyone; however, many women who previously had problems sleeping now find that it's worse.

Hormones

Surging hormones are the primary cause of sleep problems during the first trimester. During pregnancy, your body produces increasing amounts of progesterone, estrogen, and prolactin. Progesterone is essential to maintain pregnancy. Unfortunately, though, it contributes to your feeling sleepy during the day, sleep disruption, feelings of nausea, and even the need to urinate more frequently. Progesterone decreases REM sleep (active, dreaming sleep) and increases non-REM sleep.

Estrogen, too, is essential in the maintenance of pregnancy and the maturing of the fetus. It also regulates your body's production of progesterone. Estrogen can decrease REM sleep and contribute to the development of obstructive sleep apnea (see chapter 9). And finally, during pregnancy, prolactin levels increase 10 to 20 times their normal levels. Prolactin is essential in the stimulation of the production of breast milk. Prolactin, though, increases non-REM slow wave sleep.

Nausea and Morning Sickness

Linda, now on her third pregnancy, couldn't believe how nauseous she felt all the time. She had never had any morning sickness when she was pregnant with her first two children and was now totally surprised by it. But she found that if she snacked on something small just about every hour, she felt much better. She even found that munching on a cracker or two before even opening her eyes in the morning helped.

Unfortunately, morning sickness doesn't just happen in the morning. Many women feel nauseous at all times throughout the day, others just in the evenings. As one expectant mom said, "They shouldn't call it morning sickness, they should call it morning-afternoon-night sickness." Being nauseous at night can interrupt your sleep in many ways. It can make it hard for you to fall asleep. Nausea can also wake you up in the middle of the night or even in the early morning, before you are ready to get up for the day. No one knows for sure what causes first trimester nausea, but there are probably multiple factors, including rapidly increasing hormones, an increased sense of smell and sensitivity to odors, and a more sensitive stomach.

WHAT YOU CAN DO. If you are nauseous in the evening, have a bland snack, such as crackers or a banana, right before bedtime. A light snack may settle your stomach and make it easier to fall asleep. Keep snacks by your bed for middle-of-the-night or morning nausea—again, crackers can help tremendously. If you awaken nauseous in the morning, eat some crackers and then lie in bed for another 20 to 30 minutes before you actually get up.

There are other dietary changes that can help, too. Avoid fatty foods for dinner, as they can take longer to digest. Spicy, acidic, and fried foods may also upset your stomach. Some women find things like acupressure wristbands can help. Others find that ginger reduces nausea.

Luckily, morning sickness usually eases up rather quickly. About half of all women get relief from the nausea by 14 weeks, and most are no longer nauseous by 18 to 20 weeks. If you are having real difficulty with nausea, however, be sure and talk to your doctor or midwife. There are medications available, as well as more "natural" solutions such as ginger and acupressure. Managing the nausea will make it easier for you to sleep at night.

Potty Time . . . All the Time

Needing to go the bathroom is a common part of pregnancy. There are many reasons that you frequently feel the need to urinate during the first trimester of pregnancy. The hormone progesterone is one culprit. Progesterone, which your body is creating in ever-increasing amounts, affects smooth muscles in your body, making you feel that you need to pee more often. Also, as your uterus starts to expand, it will press down on your bladder. Luckily, the uterus moves above your bladder during the second trimester of pregnancy, but as it keeps expanding during pregnancy it will press on your bladder again during the third trimester. Another reason is that your kidneys are working overtime to flush out all the extra fluids that are created during pregnancy. Unfortunately, you'll need to go to the bathroom more often at night, too, which means disrupted sleep.

WHAT YOU CAN DO. To improve your sleep, try limiting your fluid intake during the evening, while being sure not to cut back on the total amount of fluids you drink for the entire day. In addition, every time you use the bathroom, be sure to completely empty your bladder. Cutting out caffeine can also help (many doctors believe that a cup of coffee or a can of soda every day while pregnant is fine). Finally, try not to wake yourself up too much when you use the bathroom during the night. Keep the lights dim. Installing a dimmer switch on your bathroom light can be a great investment of just a few dollars. Also, head right back to bed. Try not to look in on an older child, turn on the television, or check e-mail during the night when you are heading to and from the bathroom. Avoiding these activities, which can be alerting can help you fall right back to sleep.

Difficulty Finding a Comfy Sleep Position

Rebecca, only 3 weeks pregnant, was stunned at how uncomfortable it already was to sleep on her stomach given her tender breasts. She wondered how she was going to manage an entire nine months of sleeping on her side. At first she tried using an extra pillow between her legs, but she still couldn't get comfortable. She finally got a body pillow that she could drape her entire body over. It wasn't perfect, but it did help her to get more comfortable at night.

As you have quickly discovered, even in the first few months of pregnancy, it can be hard to find a comfortable sleep position. Most women don't realize that it's not just a bulging belly that makes this difficult. Tender breasts can hurt when you are sleeping on your stomach. For some women, this is the first sign of knowing that they are pregnant.

During pregnancy it is best to sleep on your side, primarily your left side. This position will become more important later on to improve the flow of blood and nutrients to your fetus and uterus and to help your kidneys get rid of waste and fluids. If you can, start getting used to it now while you can still move around easily. Sleeping on your stomach will put pressure on your belly (not an issue until you are much further along in your pregnancy) and on your breasts. Sleeping on your back may not be comfortable either, as it can lead to backaches, difficulties breathing, and in some cases decreased blood pressure. Circulation also isn't at its best when you are sleeping on your back.

WHAT YOU CAN DO. Experiment, experiment, experiment. Your first trimester is the perfect time to start training yourself to sleep on your left side. The sooner you get used to this position, the better you'll be able to sleep when your belly is bulging. So try tucking a pillow between your legs. Put another one under your belly. Try a body pillow. There are even special maternity pillows that you can purchase (see chapter 3). Some women find that sleeping in a recliner is the most comfortable, although this is much more likely later on in your pregnancy.

Common Early-Pregnancy Sleep Disorders

DURING PREGNANCY, MANY women develop sleep disorders that they never had before. Or if you already experience sleep problems, these may become much worse now that you are pregnant. The three most common sleep disorders that develop during pregnancy are insomnia, restless legs syndrome (RLS), and snoring/obstructive sleep apnea. Insomnia is likely early on in your pregnancy, whereas RLS and breathing problems during sleep usually develop later. If you think that you are having any of these sleep problems, see chapters 7 through 9 for lots of information.

. . .

> ## First Trimester Sleep Schedule
>
> **NIGHTTIME.** Schedule plenty of time for sleep—aim for nine hours. Move up your bedtime to 9:00 or 9:30—there will even be nights that you will find yourself crashing in bed by 8:00. It is better to plan to go to bed early rather than fall asleep on the couch. You'll be much more comfortable and will get a better night's sleep if you don't have to get up later just to head to bed.
>
> **DAYTIME.** Add a nap to your schedule. If you are a stay-at-home mom, try to grab some rest time when your other children are having their nap or taking a video break. Scheduling rest time for everyone is a good idea. If you work, taking a break to sit in a quiet area and close your eyes for just 15 minutes can make a big difference.

Sleepy, Fatigued . . . and Just Plain Tired

Stacia always had an overwhelming amount of energy. Her husband even called her the "Energizer Bunny," since she was constantly on the go. Everyone was surprised when Stacia began to take a nap when she got home from work and when she passed on organizing her company's holiday party. She just couldn't muster up the energy to do it once she was pregnant.

EXPECT TO BE tired during your first trimester. In the land of sleep research, we differentiate between feeling sleepy and feeling fatigued (or tired). *Sleepiness* is a need to fall asleep. So if you are sleepy and lying on the couch watching television, you'll fall asleep. On the other hand, *fatigue* is not having the energy or motivation to do anything. In this case, you'll lie on the couch channel-surfing all day but won't actually fall asleep. When you are pregnant, you'll likely feel both sleepiness and fatigue. There are a number of reasons for these feelings.

- **PROGESTERONE.** The main reason for feeling sleepy and so tired is progesterone. Progesterone is essential to maintain pregnancy, but it also causes women to feel sleepier and more tired than ever. Progesterone seems to be a soporific, meaning that it induces sleep. It also makes you have a need for more sleep.
- **LESS DEEP SLEEP.** Another thing that happens during pregnancy is that women get less deep sleep, which is related to increasing levels of estrogen. Deep sleep helps you feel awake and alert. So not getting as much deep sleep is going to make you feel less refreshed when you get up in the morning. Unfortunately, there is nothing that you can do to literally increase the amount of deep sleep that you get.
- **YOUR BODY IS WORKING FOR TWO.** Your body is working overtime right now to nurture not just yourself but also your developing baby. This means that your heart has to work more to produce extra blood. Your circulatory system is also working extra hard, carrying oxygen and nutrients to your baby.

HOW LONG IS IT GOING TO LAST? No, you won't be tired forever. Your overwhelming fatigue will lift as time goes on, but it could be a few months. You'll be surprised one day to realize that you feel like your old self!

WHAT YOU CAN DO. Although nothing is going to completely alleviate your feeling tired and exhausted, there are some things that you can do to manage overwhelming sleepiness.

- **REST.** This seems obvious, but taking a nap or heading to bed early really is the best solution for feeling sleepy. So take a nap when you can. Even a 15-minute nap can make a world of difference. Some women head to their car for a quick nap in the middle of their day when they work, if they don't have a separate office with a door that closes.

- **GET HELP.** Ask your partner to pitch in and help out. Ask a close friend or neighbor to pick up some extra groceries when she heads to the grocery store. This may be the time to splurge on getting a cleaning service. You need all the rest you can get.

- **ADJUST YOUR SCHEDULE.** Cut back on evening activities. See if you can do flex time at work, or take work home on weekends. Take a vacation or a sick day in the middle of the week.

- **DO THE MINIMUM.** This is not the time to volunteer to organize your child's class picnic or be the one to host the next event of your book club. Instead, offer to supply all the paper goods or send juice boxes. Decide to have your book club meet at a coffeehouse instead of at your house so you don't have to worry about cleaning up. Better yet, if you're really tired, just skip it.

- **EXERCISE.** Although you are feeling extra tired, exercise can help you feel more alert and energetic. You don't need to do a Pilates class three times a week or stick to your 20-mile-a-week running schedule. Instead, take a 15- or 30-minute walk. Of course, be sure to check with your doctor regarding what exercises and how much are best for you while you are pregnant.

- **EAT HEALTHILY.** Getting plenty of foods that are high in iron and protein can help you feel better. So eat foods like red meat, eggs, and chicken. Eat iron-fortified cereals and whole grains. Include fruit and yogurt in your diet. You likely know that you need extra calories now that you are pregnant. Make them good calories, though, rather than junk like potato chips. Also, be sure that you drink plenty of water.

- **THINGS TO AVOID.** When you are feeling sleepy, there are some things that you shouldn't do. You shouldn't push yourself—it's not good for you or for your developing baby. Don't rely on caffeine (a cup of coffee or a can of caffeinated soda can be a quick pick-me-up, especially in the morning, but check with your doctor first). Don't drive long distances when you are tired. Drowsy-driving accidents are serious and you can fall asleep at the wheel before you know it.

Take a Nap

NAPS ARE NOT just for babies—they're for pregnant women, too! Naps are great when you are feeling extra sleepy or you need to catch up on missed sleep from the night before. You'll have to experiment a bit, but usually a short nap is best. For some women, this is literally just a 15-minute nap; others do best with 30 to 45 minutes. Many people find that taking a nap for longer than an hour makes them feel groggy and worse than not taking a nap at all. However, try not to nap if it interferes with your sleep at night, such as making it difficult for you to fall asleep or making it more likely you'll wake up during the night. For newly pregnant women, this is less of a problem, as you need so much sleep anyway. However, if you take a nap too late in the afternoon or early afternoon, it can definitely make it hard to fall asleep at bedtime. In that case, it is better to head to bed by 9:00 p.m.

Pregnancy the Second, Third, or Fourth Time Around

Rhonda found that being pregnant the second time around was much harder. Being pregnant again was wonderful, but different. This time she had a 19-month-old to run after, more housework, and more driving to and from work and day care. She had less time to focus on the pregnancy and the new baby than she had had the first time.

DEALING WITH FEELING sleep deprived or not getting a good night's sleep when you are pregnant with your first child is hard. However, dealing with it when you are pregnant for the second, third, or fourth time and have older children at home is even harder. When you are pregnant for the first time, it is much easier to grab a catnap during the middle of the day or when you first get home from work. Heading to bed early is not too difficult either. These things may become impossible if you have other children. And compounding the issue is the energy it takes to keep up with kids. Two-year-olds just don't understand the words "but Mommy is too tired" when they want you to play a seventh round of ring-around-the-rosy. Keeping up with a toddler when you are feeling exhausted already, or still waking up during the night with a 3-year-old, can compound the overwhelming fatigue.

WHAT YOU CAN DO. Although it may never be perfect, there are things that you can do to help you get the rest you need when you have other children at home. Hire a babysitter or sign your child up for a few hours of preschool at least a few days a week. Institute an hour or two of quiet time in the afternoon for everyone. Little ones can head for a nap, while older ones can do quiet activities, such as color or watch a favorite television show that you taped. Yes, we all know that limiting television is a good thing, but the reality is that everyone needs some down time, especially moms!

Cope with Life's Demands

YOU MAY FIND that you are having a hard time coping with life's demands, especially if you are having problems sleeping at night or are feeling tired during the day. At this time, it is key that you focus on yourself, ensuring that you stay healthy and take care not only of yourself but also of your developing baby. Prioritizing all of the things that you have to do and getting help are going to ensure that you are able to cope. Here are some other things that can help:

- Figure out during what part of the day you are at your best. At that time of the day, do the work that requires the most brainpower. At other times of the day, do things that take less brainpower, such as returning phone calls or checking e-mail.
- Rather than think about things that need to be done as massive projects, break them down into manageable pieces. For example, it can be overwhelming to think about getting the baby's room ready if you are starting from scratch. Instead, take it in small steps: (1) get the room painted, (2) buy curtains, (3) hang curtains, (4) set up the crib, and so on. Does getting your taxes done seem insurmountable? Again, think of it in steps, each one manageable: (1) buy a computer tax program, (2) enter your W-2 forms, (3) find the mortgage and property tax receipts, (4) enter the mortgage and property tax receipts, and so on. Each step should be

one that takes only 10 or 15 minutes. If you get one step done a day, that's great. If you get two or more steps done, think of all the things that you can cross off your to-do list!

- Find someone to help you with a task. Many things that are exhausting and overwhelming if you do them alone can become fun when doing them with someone else. Invite a friend over to help empty the final boxes that you never managed to unpack. Order in pizza and make it a social occasion. Have several girlfriends over to have a "decorate the nursery" or "paint my kitchen" party. You'll find that your friends won't mind, especially as it's so much easier to help someone else with a tedious task than do your own chores. At the same time, you'll have fun and get to spend time together.

Solve Sleep Problems in Older Children Now

Diana's 19-month-old son still awoke at least once every night, and her 5-year-old would end up in their bed in the middle of the night at least once or twice a week. She had no idea how she was going to handle it when the new baby arrived.

Far too often, families wait to handle an older child's sleep problems until just before the new baby is due. Don't wait until you are 7 or 8 months pregnant to solve a sleep problem of an older child. It is much better and easier to do it now before the baby is born and you have two little ones up during the night. There are many resources available, including my parenting books *Sleeping Through the Night: How Infants, Toddlers, and*

Their Parents Can Get a Good Night's Sleep for children up to age 3, and *Take Charge of Your Child's Sleep: The All-in-One Resource for Solving Sleep Problems in Kids and Teens* for ages 3 to 18. Develop a plan now, be consistent, and you'll have everyone sleeping well before the arrival of the new baby.

First Trimester Sleep Tips

- **MAKE SLEEP A PRIORITY.** Plan for sleep. Make a schedule for sleep. Put sleep on your to-do list!

- **SLEEP WHENEVER AND WHEREVER.** Sleep is important during pregnancy, so don't resist the urge. Grab a catnap or settle in for a long afternoon's snooze.

- **GET COMFY.** Find a comfy position to sleep in during the night. This may require using extra pillows. You may find that sleeping on your side is the most comfortable.

- **DIM THE LIGHTS.** During the night, if you need to get up, use a nightlight or install dimmer switches. The less light, the easier it will be to get back to sleep.

- **KEEP SNACKS BY YOUR BEDSIDE.** Keep bland snacks, like crackers, by your bed to combat nausea at bedtime, in the middle of the night, or first thing in the morning.

- **CUT BACK ON FLUIDS IN THE EVENING.** If you are waking up throughout the night to pee, cut back on fluids in the evening before bedtime, although be sure to keep up your fluid intake throughout the rest of the day.

. . .

Reminders

- There are many common causes of sleep problems during the first trimester, including surging hormones, morning sickness, middle-of-the-night trips to the bathroom, and difficulty finding a comfortable position.
- Be sure to schedule plenty of time for sleep, including heading to bed early and planning time for a nap.
- Feeling tired all the time? Be sure to rest as much as possible, exercise, eat healthily, and plan to only do the minimum.
- If you have other children who are having problems sleeping, solve those sleep issues now instead of waiting until right before the new baby arrives.

FIVE

The Second Trimester

*"I finally feel human again, but now
I'm waking up with excruciating leg cramps."*
—Ronnie, 23 weeks pregnant

*"I sailed through the first trimester, feeling great and
sleeping well. Now I'm having problems sleeping,
right at the time that all the books say
I should be feeling at my best."*
—Melissa, 17 weeks pregnant

The second trimester is often called the "honeymoon" period. It's the time when most women feel their best during pregnancy. You may now have the "looking great, feeling great" pregnancy glow. Most concerns about miscarriage have passed and you are likely feeling less nauseous and more energetic.

For many women, the second trimester is a time when sleep problems temporarily subside, although there are some women who find that their sleep is even more disrupted now than during the first trimester. Sleep issues that you may experience during this trimester include the need to change your sleep position, increasing discomfort, continuing need to urinate, and starting to feel the baby move. Other common pregnancy ailments may develop that interfere with sleep, such as nighttime leg cramps, back pain that makes it even harder to find a comfortable sleep position, and increasing nasal congestion.

But first, the good news . . .

The Good News

AS MENTIONED, THE second trimester is when most women look and feel their best during pregnancy. There are usually fewer concerns about your baby during the second trimester, and you've likely gotten used to the idea that you will soon have another member of your family. The same is true for sleep. Most women sleep their best during the second trimester and feel better. There are a number of reasons:

- **FEWER TRIPS TO THE BATHROOM.** During the second tri-mester, your uterus moves up from the pelvis and into your abdomen, so there is much less pressure on your bladder. Now that your bladder (temporarily) is no longer being compressed by your developing baby, you won't need to go to the bathroom as often, which means less waking to go pee in the middle of the night.
- **HORMONES ARE LEVELING OFF.** Although your body is still producing progesterone, the levels are rising more slowly, so you are not feeling as sleepy during the day.
- **MORNING SICKNESS SUBSIDES.** Most women find that any morning sickness they experienced during the first trimester starts to dissipate during the second trimester. This will help you feel more yourself during the day and help you sleep better at night. A warning, though: a few women experience morning sickness throughout much of their pregnancy. However, this is quite rare.

- **LESS DESIRE TO NAP DURING THE DAY.** Just as you are likely sleeping better at night, you are also likely feeling more energetic during the day. Most women do not feel the overwhelming fatigue at this point in their pregnancy as they did during the first trimester. You may be amazed to be feeling yourself again, with your old energy. Most women also feel less of a need to nap during the day. As important as it was to nap early on in your pregnancy, it may have also interfered with your nighttime sleep. So with fewer daytime naps you are also likely falling asleep faster and staying asleep during the night.

Don't Be Fooled . . . You Still Need Lots of Sleep

ALTHOUGH YOU ARE likely feeling much more energetic and more like yourself, don't try to pack it all in and try to do everything. Your body is still working overtime and you need to keep getting your rest. That includes getting lots of sleep at night and continuing to nap if you need the extra sleep.

. . . And Now for the Bad News

ALTHOUGH YOU ARE likely feeling more energetic and sleeping better at night during the second trimester, there are sleep issues that may continue or may develop during the second trimester. The recent National Sleep Foundation's *Sleep in America Poll 2007* indicates that many women are having problems sleeping during these months.

GETTING A GOOD NIGHT'S SLEEP. Only 28 percent of pregnant women in their second trimester report that they get a good night's sleep every night or almost every night, and 30 percent state that they get a good night's sleep only a few nights a month or less.

SLEEP PROBLEMS. Sleep problems are very common during the second trimester. Most women (83 percent) report symptoms of insomnia, with the majority of women (72 percent) waking often during the night. Fewer women (32 percent) have problems falling asleep or waking too early and not being able to fall back to sleep (45 percent). One-third of women snore at least a few nights a week (see chapter 9), and 17 percent report symptoms consistent with restless legs syndrome (see chapter 8).

DAYTIME SLEEPINESS. About one in four women (26 percent) report experiencing daytime sleepiness at least a few days a week, and 23 percent report a high likelihood of dozing during the day. One out of ten women (11 percent) state that they have missed at least one day of work in the past month because of sleep, or lack thereof, and one out of three drove drowsy at least once in the past month.

Second Trimester Sleep Schedule

NIGHTTIME. Continue to schedule plenty of time for sleep. You may now be able to stay up closer to your usual bedtime, but don't stay up too late. Stick with a bedtime of 10:00 or 10:30 to ensure that you get at least 8 hours of sleep.

DAYTIME. Feel free to continue taking a nap. Naps can be refreshing and help you get the sleep that you need. Don't nap too late in the day, though, or else you may have a hard time falling asleep at bedtime.

Sleep Problems During the Second Trimester

National Sleep Foundation's *Sleep in America Poll 2007*

Sleep issue	Percentage of pregnant women
Get a good night's sleep every night or almost every night	28
Insomnia	83
Waking often at night	72
Problems falling asleep	32
Waking too early and not being able to fall back to sleep	45
Snore	33
Restless legs syndrome	17
Daytime sleepiness	26
High likelihood of dozing during the day	23
Missed work because of sleep issue	11

Causes of Sleep Problems During the Second Trimester

JUST AS DURING the first trimester, there are many different reasons why you may not be sleeping well during the second trimester. Below are just some of these possibilities and what you can do about them.

Trouble Finding a Comfortable Sleep Position

You may have been able to continue to sleep on your stomach up to this point, but that's probably now changing. As your belly starts getting bigger, you'll find that it gets harder to find a comfortable sleep position, although stomach sleeping is not a danger to your developing baby.

WHAT YOU CAN DO. If you haven't already, now is a good time to start getting used to sleeping on your left side. It's best for your baby, as it increases the amount of blood and nutrients to your developing fetus. Also, your liver is on your right side, so lying on your left side keeps your uterus off your liver. And it is likely the most comfortable position during the night. However, don't worry about it too much, as you will roll over at times during the night.

A pillow under your belly and one between your legs can help. Body pillows and specially designed maternity pillows are also good choices. Some women even make the switch to sleeping in a recliner during their second trimester.

Your Baby Is On the Move

MOST WOMEN START to feel the first movements of their baby between 16 and 22 weeks. For women who have been pregnant before, you may notice it even earlier, as you know what it feels like. Some women describe these first kicks as a fluttering feeling, almost like butterflies. Your baby has actually been quite active for weeks and weeks, but your baby is so small that it takes awhile until you can feel the movements. At first you may think that the movements you feel are gas or other stomach rumblings, but you'll come to realize when it is the baby. Feeling your baby move is definitely one of the best parts of pregnancy.

One of the best times to feel your baby move is when you are lying in bed at night. There are fewer distractions of the day and it's a quiet time for you and your baby. Those beginning baby movements can even keep you up at night. Let's face it—it's just so cool!

Leg Cramps

Meg is pregnant with her third child. The aspect of pregnancy that she dreads the most is the thought of starting to wake up with excruciating leg cramps. It didn't happen often with her first pregnancy, but it was terrible during her second. Starting in her second trimester, she woke up almost every night with a leg cramp. She began to dread going to bed. Luckily, she hasn't started having them yet this time around, but she worries about when they will start.

Sleeping for Three or More

IT'S HARD ENOUGH to be pregnant with one baby, let alone if you are having twins, triplets, or more! You may not find that the second trimester is as much of a honeymoon period, primarily because there is more baby, making you less comfortable. Being pregnant with multiples also means that you are more likely to become iron deficient, which may mean the development of restless legs syndrome (see chapter 8). You are also much more likely to be put on bed rest. Chapter 6 provides detailed information about bed rest. It may be worth your reading this section now, in case you suddenly need to go on bed rest or stay in the hospital.

The first time that you wake up with a sudden jolt as a result of a leg cramp can be quite a surprising (and painful!) experience. You may also become wary of sleeping, worried that you are going to have another cramp while you sleep. Leg cramps often develop during the second trimester of pregnancy as calcium levels in your body decrease.

WHAT YOU CAN DO. Try doing leg stretches before you go to bed at night. Regular exercise may also help. During a leg cramp, some women find that applying heat can help, as well as massaging the area. In addition, sleeping with heavy covers can make leg cramps worse, either because it restricts movement or just from the sheer weight of the covers. So try to use lighter covers if you can. If you are having frequent leg cramps, more information on this is provided in chapter 6.

Jolene found that at least once a week she got excruciating leg cramps in the middle of the night. The more she thought about it, the more she realized that she usually woke up with leg cramps on Thursday or Friday nights, after a long week of work and not exercising. She was much more likely to work out on the weekends and earlier in the week, before the week got too busy. She began heading to the gym more and found that it made a big difference.

Back Pain

Suzanne was 26 years old and pregnant for the first time. She was extremely surprised when she starting having back pain, as she had never had it before. She had always associated back pain with being older or being injured. Luckily, the pain was intermittent—some days her back hurt and others it felt fine.

Back pain is part of being pregnant for many women. Studies find that between 50 and 80 percent of women experience back pain during pregnancy. As your baby grows and your uterus expands, your center of gravity will shift, putting a strain on your back. In addition, increasing weight, stretching and weakening of your abdominal muscles, and hormones causing your joints and ligaments to loosen will all contribute to back pain. You may feel back pain throughout the day or just at night after a long day. Pain triggers may include walking, sitting for long periods, lying in bed, rolling over, getting up from a chair, or lifting things (especially toddlers who still insist on being carried everywhere!).

There are some women who are more likely to develop back pain. Obviously, if you experienced back pain before, you are more likely to have it now that you are pregnant. Women carrying multiples are also more likely to have back pain, given that they are carrying around more weight and their uterus is expanding more quickly. Also, the less active you are and the less you exercise, the greater your risk. Weaker stomach and back muscles are going to lead to more pain. There are also many different kinds of back pain, including lumbar pain (lower back pain) and posterior pelvic pain (lower than lumbar pain, often in your bottom or the back of your thighs).

WHAT YOU CAN DO TO AVOID DEVELOPING BACK PAIN. Fortunately, there are things that you can do to avoid developing back pain in the first place and to minimize it once you start having pain. An excellent first step is to work on strengthening the muscles of your back, legs, and stomach. If you haven't exercised in years, start off slow. Trying to do 100 sit-ups and 100 leg lifts on your very first day of exercise is going to cause pain, not avoid it! Be sure to stretch before any exercise, but do so gently so that you don't pull anything. Consider the best exercises for you, especially now that you are pregnant. Yoga and swimming are two excellent choices for pregnant women. You may wish to investigate whether there are any exercise classes available in your area that are specifically for pregnant women.

There are other things that you can do to avoid back pain. If you are going to be sitting for long stretches of time, sit up straight. Support your feet with a footstool and take frequent breaks. Get up and walk around at least once every hour.

There are also many back support devices available on the market, and even stores that specialize in products to alleviate back pain.

Not only should you sit up straight, but you should also stand up straight. This may be hard to do when you feel as if you have a watermelon strapped to your belly, but it will help keep your spine aligned and put less strain on your back. Try also not to stand for long periods. Just as with sitting, take breaks from standing.

Other small changes can make a huge difference. Don't carry heavy things. Have the grocery store pack your purchases in several small bags rather than one big heavy bag. Carry equal weight in both hands to balance out your body. In addition, avoid high heels, especially if they put strain on your back. And don't reach for high objects. That's an easy way to pull a muscle in your back.

To help you sleep, try sleeping on your side with one or both knees bent. Put a pillow between your knees. Add another pillow under your belly. Getting out of bed can be hard on your back. To help yourself get out of bed without hurting your back, first roll to your side, bending your legs at your knees and hips. Then swing your legs over the side of the bed. Finally, use your arms to push yourself up.

WHAT YOU CAN DO TO HELP BACK PAIN. There are a number of things that you can do to alleviate back pain if it has already developed. Some women find that heat helps, whereas others find cold to be effective. Try a warm bath or a heating pad for heat, or a cold pack for cold. Heat is usually more effective, at least in providing temporary relief. Massage also can help. Many massage therapists are trained in prenatal massage, or you can learn about different massage techniques and see what feels best.

Finally, limit your activities, especially those that cause pain, such as climbing stairs or carrying heavy objects. Certain household chores, such as vacuuming and mopping, can contribute to back pain. Make sure that you take it easy. There are also many exercises that you can do to help with back pain. Talk to your doctor or a pregnancy exercise specialist about what exercises would be best for you and for the kind of back pain that you are experiencing.

Round Ligament Pain

Sarah panicked the first time that she experienced round ligament pain. She had rolled over in bed one morning and experienced a shooting pain in her right side. She immediately called her doctor, who saw her right away. He reassured her that she was not miscarrying; it was simply round ligament pain. She continued to have these pains whenever she got up too suddenly from a chair or rolled over too quickly.

Round ligament pain is something that you have likely never heard of before, but it can happen during pregnancy, usually during the second trimester. Round ligament pain is a brief, sharp stabbing pain in the lower abdomen or groin. This pain usually occurs suddenly and often happens when you change position, especially getting out of bed or a chair. It can happen at other times, too, such as when you cough or roll over in bed. It can also feel like a dull ache that lasts longer, which may occur if you've been walking a lot.

The round ligament holds your uterus in suspension in your abdomen. As your baby grows and the uterus expands, this causes a stretching and thinning of the round ligament. This ligament can go into spasm, which causes the sudden sharp pain. These pains are more common on the right side because of the way the uterus usually turns.

WHAT YOU CAN DO. Resting and relaxing is one of the best things that you can do for the pain. During a round ligament pain, try flexing your knees up to your belly or lie on your side with pillows supporting your belly and between your legs. Applying heat, such as a warm bath or a heating pad, can also help. If the pain occurs when you are lying down, try lying on your opposite side. Change how you move, trying not to move suddenly. Getting up from bed or from a chair slowly can decrease the likelihood of a spasm.

If your pain is usually associated with being active, you may need to cut back for a while. Once the pain eases, you can slowly return to your usual level of exercise and activity. Fortunately, round ligament pain gets better as pregnancy progresses, so this is not something that you will likely need to live with for long.

There are many other things that can cause abdominal pain, so discuss your symptoms with your doctor. Be sure and contact your doctor right away, especially if you are also having any fever, chills, bleeding, pain on urination, or difficulty walking.

Nasal Congestion

Nasal congestion is quite common during pregnancy, affecting about 20 to 30 percent of women. Having a stuffy noise can cause sleep problems, especially as your stuffy nose may get worse when you are lying down at night. You may keep waking up throughout the night, as it may be harder for you to breathe, just as when you have a cold.

This nasal congestion may be due to allergies or a cold, but often it is simply related to being pregnant. Like so many other things during pregnancy, this nasal congestion is due to hormones, in this case estrogen. Estrogen leads to swelling of the mucous membranes in your nose. In addition, estrogen makes you produce more mucus. Increased blood in your body and the swelling of blood vessels also contribute to nasal congestion.

There are a few ways to help you differentiate between nasal congestion that is due to pregnancy and that due to a cold or allergies. If you are also sneezing, coughing, and don't feel well overall, then your stuffy nose is likely related to a cold or some other illness. If you are also sneezing and have itchy eyes, then it's likely related to allergies. If you have none of these, just a stuffy nose, then it's most likely pregnancy related.

WHAT YOU CAN DO. There are several things that you can do to alleviate a stuffy noise, especially at night when it can interfere with your sleep. First of all, during the night elevate your head. You can do this by adding an extra pillow or two, raising one end of your bed, or in severe cases sleeping in a recliner chair. Drink lots of fluid during the day to keep yourself hydrated, which will also help your nasal congestion. Steam can help, so try taking a warm shower or sitting in a steamy bathroom.

Saline nose sprays can improve nasal congestion, as can running a humidifier or vaporizer, especially at night. Avoid anything that you may be allergic to, such as strong perfumes or scents. Install an air purifier in your bedroom to help control allergens so that you can sleep better. Cigarette smoke can also make it worse, so ban smokers from your home. There are also decongestants available that can help with nasal congestion. Check with your doctor before using one, though, to be sure that it is safe to use during pregnancy.

Cindy was 27-weeks pregnant and felt like she'd had a cold forever. She realized that she felt fine other than not being able to breathe through her nose. To help the nasal congestion, she began using a saline spray at bedtime and put humidifiers in her bedroom and her family room. Although it didn't completely solve the problem, it helped a great deal.

Luckily, once the baby is born, nasal congestion related to pregnancy clears up either right away or within a few weeks.

Itchy Skin

Itchy skin is quite common during pregnancy, especially on your belly and breasts. Much of this itchiness comes from your skin stretching in these two areas. Hormones, primarily estrogen, may also contribute to feeling itchy during pregnancy. Other areas of your body that may itch include your palms and soles of your feet. In addition, problems like dry skin and eczema that you had before can get worse during pregnancy.

For Shana, the itchiness started right around the time she was 5 months pregnant. She started taking oatmeal baths at night, slathering her body with moisturizer whenever she got a chance, and put a vaporizer in both her office and her bedroom. Although it didn't solve the problem completely, she felt much better after about a week.

WHAT YOU CAN DO. There are a number of things that you can do to alleviate the itching. Avoid hot showers and baths; instead it is better to take a bath or a shower that is shorter and cooler. Hot showers and baths can dry out your skin and make the itching worse. A warm oatmeal bath can also help. Use a mild soap, one without any fragrances or other additives that may be drying. Rinse off well at the end of your shower or bath. After you get out of the shower, pat dry and don't rub. Rubbing can remove naturally produced oils on your skin. Follow this by slathering yourself with a moisturizer. It's best to do this then when your skin is still moist. Continue to slather yourself several times a day with a moisturizer, avoiding those with scents, as they can cause irritation.

During the day, wear loose cotton clothing. Avoid going out in the heat when it is hot outside, as it can make the itching worse. During the winter months turn on a humidifier, especially in your bedroom at night. The dry air from heating your home, especially if you have a forced-air heating system, can really dry out your skin and make you feel itchy.

Be sure to drink plenty of water during the day. Drinking water will ensure that you do not get dehydrated. Also use a lip balm, especially at night when you sleep. Licking your lips will actually make them drier, so it is much better to use a balm.

Heartburn and Reflux

As your baby develops and you start getting bigger, you may find that you begin to have heartburn and/or reflux. As your uterus enlarges, it presses up on your diaphragm and displaces your intestines and the bottom of your esophagus. These can contribute to developing reflux and heartburn. These symptoms are more common during the third trimester, although they can definitely develop during the second trimester.

WHAT YOU CAN DO. There are many relatively simple treatments for heartburn and reflux. Chapter 6 provides more extensive information on this topic.

Vivid Dreams and Nightmares

Stephanie was 5 months pregnant with her first child. She began having more vivid dreams than she could ever recall. Most of the dreams related to her having the baby prematurely and someone taking the baby away before she got a chance to see it. Some dreams were about other unusual, frightening experiences. One night she had a nightmare that she was being stabbed by a butcher knife. Another night she dreamed that her husband had fallen off a cliff.

Lisa, too, kept having the same recurring dream. In the dream her baby was born with a huge head and an extremely tiny body. She kept waking up horrified, wondering if this was a sign that there was something wrong with the baby or that she wouldn't love the baby.

Many women report that they seem to dream more frequently and more vividly while they are pregnant. As you might expect, many of these dreams are about pregnancy, but not all. Women report dreaming about horrible things happening to them or loved ones, an increasing number of erotic dreams, and dreams that simply do not make sense. Dreaming about leaving the baby behind, inadvertently injuring the baby, or even something more frightening happening to the baby are all common. Don't worry. These dreams are perfectly normal, and nightmares are especially common. You may also dream intensely about the joys of being a mom, cuddling a brand-new baby, or celebrating your child's first steps. Some women like to keep a journal of their dreams to read later on or to share with their partner.

There are two biological reasons for this increased, vivid dreaming. One is that sleep is more often disrupted and thus women are more likely to recall their dreams. Additionally, studies have found increased REM sleep during pregnancy, which is the stage of sleep when dreaming occurs.

Not only do pregnant women dream more during this time, so do their partners. Soon-to-be dads may dream about becoming a dad and about their developing baby. Just as with women, these dreams can be either wonderful ones about their baby or frightening ones.

Dan woke up in a sweat with his heart pounding. He had been dreaming that he was in a store and realized that his baby had disappeared. When he woke up, he wondered if this dream was a sign that he wasn't ready to become a father and whether he was responsible enough to take on caring for a baby.

Common Mid-Pregnancy Sleep Disorders

DURING THE SECOND trimester, many women develop sleep problems that are beyond the simple annoyances. Insomnia, restless legs syndrome, snoring, and sleep apnea are all common. So if you are having major problems sleeping at night, don't be surprised. Even the best of sleepers can develop a sleep disorder while they are pregnant. Luckily, these problems usually resolve after the baby is born.

Insomnia

Insomnia goes beyond just having problems sleeping at night. Insomnia involves problems falling asleep and/or staying asleep most nights.

WHAT YOU CAN DO. To help you determine whether you have insomnia, and for lots of information on ways to manage your problems sleeping, see chapter 7. Basic sleep strategies are provided, as well as behavioral treatments that have been proven to improve insomnia.

Restless Legs Syndrome

Do your legs bother you while you are trying to fall asleep or when you are sitting still for long periods? Restless legs syndrome (RLS) is an uncomfortable sensation in your legs that many women describe as creepy-crawly or like bugs under the skin. Moving your legs will make the sensations better, but only momentarily.

WHAT YOU CAN DO. Chapter 8 provides extensive information on RLS and ways to help you both improve the symptoms and sleep better at night.

Snoring and Sleep Apnea

Snoring is extremely common during pregnancy. For many women, snoring is just annoying, especially to their bed partner! But for other women, snoring may be a symptom of a more serious problem called sleep apnea. Sleep apnea is a problem breathing when you sleep. Symptoms include snoring, difficulty breathing while asleep, breathing pauses, gasping, and choking.

WHAT YOU CAN DO. If you snore, or have any problems breathing while you sleep, be sure to read chapter 9 on snoring and sleep apnea. In addition, talk to your doctor about ways to treat your snoring and have an assessment done for sleep apnea.

Second Trimester Sleep Tips

- **GET YOUR 8 HOURS.** Be sure to get your 8 hours of sleep at night. Continue to make sleep a priority so that you will feel your best.
- **AVOID HEARTBURN.** Try not to eat large amounts of spicy, acidic, or fried foods. Eat smaller meals throughout the day, rather than large meals. Sleep propped up if heartburn bothers you at night.
- **FIND A COMFORTABLE POSITION.** Your second trimester is a good time to experiment with different ways to get comfortable at night. Getting used to sleeping with pillows between your legs and under your belly will help you throughout the rest of your pregnancy.
- **AVOID BACK PAIN, ESPECIALLY WHILE YOU SLEEP.** Avoid back pain by finding a comfortable sleep position that doesn't put pressure on your back. During the day, avoid sitting or standing for long periods, and limit any activities that may lead to pulled back muscles or too much strain on your spine.
- **STAY HYDRATED.** Drink lots of fluids during the day to help nasal congestion, heartburn, and itchy skin.
- **SEEK HELP FOR SLEEP PROBLEMS.** If you are having major sleep issues, talk to your doctor or midwife to help assess what is contributing to your sleep problems and develop a plan to improve your sleep.

Reminders

- Most women feel their best during the second trimester. You'll feel more energetic, less nauseous, and will

likely be sleeping better. However, don't be fooled—
you still need plenty of sleep.

- Sleep problems are still common during the second
trimester, and some women start to develop new sleep
issues, including leg cramps, restless legs syndrome,
and snoring or sleep apnea.

- Avoid back pain by strengthening your muscles
through exercise, being careful about what you pick up
and being sure to sit up and stand up straight.

- Reduce the likelihood of nasal congestion and itchy
skin by keeping hydrated, slathering yourself with
moisturizer, and avoiding allergens.

- Don't be surprised if you are having vivid dreams
(or nightmares), especially about being pregnant and
about your baby.

SIX

The Third Trimester

"I feel huge! There is no other way that I can describe it.
Huge—like a beached whale, a blimp. Just all-around big.
There is no way to get comfortable at night when you
don't feel comfortable in your own skin."
—*Elizabeth, 38 weeks pregnant*

"I just got put on bed rest and now I can't sleep at night.
I'm just so worried about the baby."
—*Amanda, 8 months pregnant*

The third trimester is when the majority of pregnant women encounter sleep problems, even if they have slept fine up to this point. For example, research shows that 97 percent of women in their third trimester wake during the night and 91 percent report restless sleep. And you'll find that you will likely wake up often—an average of three or more times per night. Two-thirds of pregnant women wake up five or more nights per week. That's a lot of wakings and a lot of disrupted nights! As you can imagine, trying to keep up with their normal schedules, struggling to stay awake, and not getting a good night's sleep result in many women feeling exhausted much of the time by the end of pregnancy.

. . .

Looking at the Numbers

THERE IS NO question that sleep is disturbed during the third trimester. The recent National Sleep Foundation's *Sleep in America Poll 2007* indicates that by this point most women are having problems sleeping.

GETTING A GOOD NIGHT'S SLEEP. Only 29 percent of pregnant women in their third trimester report that they get a good night's sleep every night or almost every night. Forty-one percent state that they get a good night's sleep only a few nights a month or less. This leaves the other 30 percent sleeping well just a few nights a week.

SLEEP PROBLEMS. Sleep problems are very common during the third trimester. Most women (84 percent) report symptoms of insomnia, with the majority of women (77 percent) waking often during the night. Fewer women (45 percent) have problems falling asleep or waking too early and not being able to fall back asleep (43 percent). One-third of women snore at least a few nights a week, and one out of every five women (20 percent) report symptoms consistent with restless legs syndrome (see chapter 8 for more information on RLS).

DAYTIME SLEEPINESS. About one in four women (27 percent) report experiencing daytime sleepiness at least a few days a week, and one out of three women (35 percent) report a high likelihood of dozing during the day. One out of about every five women (18 percent) state that they have missed at least one day of work in the past month because of sleep, or lack thereof, and one out of three drove drowsy at least once in the past month.

. . .

Sleep Problems During the Third Trimester

National Sleep Foundation's *Sleep in America Poll 2007*

Sleep issue	Percentage of pregnant women
Get a good night's sleep every night or almost every night	29
Insomnia	84
Waking often at night	77
Problems falling asleep	45
Waking too early and not being able to fall back asleep	43
Snore	33
Restless legs syndrome	20
Daytime sleepiness	27
High likelihood of dozing during the day	35
Missed work because of sleep issue	18

Causes of Sleep Problems During the Third Trimester

THERE ARE MANY reasons for your sleep to be disrupted during the third trimester. Below are a number of these reasons, and ways that you can manage them to help you get a better night's sleep.

Heartburn

After almost every meal, Joni, 8 months pregnant, would feel a burning in her chest. It got much worse at night when she was lying down, especially if she had had a large dinner. The best way to get comfortable at night was to sleep propped up on a lot of pillows. She was even resorting to sleeping in a recliner in the living room on some nights.

Heartburn is a burning sensation in your chest. It is caused by stomach acids going back up into the esophagus (the tube that carries food from your mouth). It actually has nothing to do with your heart.

More than half of all pregnant women get heartburn, and it's much more common during the third trimester. This is because as your baby gets larger and takes up more space, there is pressure on your stomach and esophagus. Your baby and expanding uterus are pushing on your stomach, moving it out of its normal position.

In addition, heartburn is caused by your digestive system not working as well during pregnancy. As with just about everything, hormones are to blame.

WHAT YOU CAN DO. There are a number of things that you can do to manage heartburn.

- **SMALLER MEALS.** One of the best ways to manage heartburn is to eat smaller meals. It is better to have five or six small meals than three large ones.
- **EAT SLOWLY.** Even if it's a small meal, eat slowly. Eating more slowly will make you feel full before you have overdone it and eaten too much.
- **AVOID CERTAIN FOODS.** There are many foods that are known to trigger heartburn, so avoid them. These include fried foods, chocolate, peppermint, garlic, and onions. Alcohol can also trigger heartburn, but you should be avoiding alcohol anyway. Coffee, too, can trigger heartburn. And finally, acidic fruit juices can lead to heartburn.

- **DRINK FLUIDS.** Plenty of fluids, especially water, can help ease and prevent heartburn. So drink lots of fluids, more during the day so that you don't have to make frequent nighttime trips to the bathroom.
- **EAT EARLY, WELL BEFORE BEDTIME.** Try to eat dinner early in the evening so that you can stay upright for several hours before heading to bed. Allowing your body to digest before lying down will help avoid heartburn. Even during the day, don't lie down for at least 30 minutes after eating.
- **PROP YOURSELF UP.** If you get heartburn every time you lie down, try raising the head of your bed. You can also prop yourself up on pillows. Some women find that their heartburn is so bad that they sleep much better in a recliner.
- **DRINK SKIM MILK.** Milk can help ease the pain of heartburn. Drink skim or low-fat milk though, instead of whole milk, to avoid the extra calories.
- **OVER-THE-COUNTER MEDICATIONS.** Over-the-counter medications, like Tums, are typically safe to take when you are pregnant and provide extra calcium. Tums, like other similar antacids, are simply calcium carbonate. Other types of antacids contain magnesium hydroxide or magnesium oxide and are also usually considered safe during pregnancy. These antacids work by neutralizing the acid in your stomach. Other antacids should be avoided during pregnancy. For example, some contain aspirin (such as Alka-Seltzer). As always, check with your doctor before using any of these medications.
- **TALK TO YOUR DOCTOR.** Your doctor can recommend other treatments for your heartburn.

Third Trimester Sleep Schedule

NIGHTTIME. IF YOU were able to return to your prepregnancy sleep schedule during your second trimester, it's likely time to return to scheduling plenty of time for sleep. Move your bedtime back to 9:00 or 9:30 again, although it is unlikely that you'll need to crash by 8:00 as you did during your first trimester. Work on creating a sleep-friendly bed for yourself, with lots of extra pillows.

DAYTIME. Adding a nap to your schedule can be quite helpful. Grabbing some shut-eye for even 15-minutes at some point in the day will help. In addition, schedule lots of rest time throughout the day. Take 5 or 10 minutes to sit down and put your feet up. This will help relieve pressure on your back and give you a few minutes' respite.

"I Just Can't Get Comfortable"

Discomfort can be the name of the game during the third trimester. Although some women sail through pregnancy never feeling uncomfortable, many women feel like a "beached whale," especially by the end of pregnancy.

Stephanie was 7 months pregnant and she already felt and looked huge. Strangers would come up to her and ask whether she was due any day. When she answered "not for another two months," they would ask whether she was having twins. Stephanie just seemed to carry big; it was the same with her other two pregnancies. By this point, she just couldn't wait to have the baby and get her body back. She was uncomfortable all the time, whether standing or sitting, and lying down at night to sleep was the worst. No matter what she did, she just couldn't get comfortable.

As your belly gets bigger, you, too, may be feeling like Stephanie. Some women feel as if they have a watermelon or beach ball strapped to their front. Having a big belly out front is definitely not conducive to finding a comfortable position to sleep. Some suggestions for finding a comfortable sleep position include the following:

- **LIE ON YOUR LEFT SIDE.** Try lying on your left side with your knees bent. The left side is usually recommended as the best sleep position during pregnancy for both you and your baby, but feel free to lie on your right side if that is more comfortable.

- **USE LOTS OF PILLOWS.** Try tucking a pillow under your belly and another one between your knees. Some women find that surrounding themselves with lots of pillows works best for them.

- **BODY PILLOW.** A body pillow can also help you get comfortable at night. Snuggle up with it, resting your belly on top of the pillow.

- **BLANKETS.** Some women find that they are much warmer during the night when they are pregnant. Try different types of blankets, such as a light blanket rather than a heavier comforter. Sleeping with a light blanket under a comforter can also do the trick. When you're cold, keep both blankets on. And when you're hot, you can simply fling off the top comforter.

- **RECLINER CHAIR.** Some women find that no matter what they do, they just can't get comfortable lying flat in a bed. If this is the case for you, try sleeping in a reclining chair. The semi-upright position may be the most comfortable for you.

Back Pain

Back pain is a common occurrence during pregnancy. One study found that 68 percent of pregnant women experienced back pain during their pregnancy, and the majority reported that it disturbed their sleep. This back pain may bother you when you are walking, standing, sitting, or lying down. Basically, it can hurt all the time.

There are several causes of back pain during pregnancy. One cause is that the ligaments between the pelvic bones soften and joints loosen. These are important changes in preparation for delivery but can be difficult in the meantime. The other primary cause is the weight of the baby and how it is distributed on your body, which will affect your posture. As your posture changes, this will put pressure on your back.

WHAT YOU CAN DO. A complete description on how to deal with back pain can be found in chapter 5. Simple things that you can do include avoiding activities that cause you pain, such as climbing stairs and lifting heavy objects, and being sure to sit and stand up straight. Get out of a bed or a chair slowly. Use a heating pad or other source of warmth to ease pain.

Baby Keeps Kicking

Rebecca was pregnant with her fourth child. She just couldn't believe how active this baby was compared to all her other children. It felt as if she was being kicked all day and all night long. The worst was when she was kicked in the bladder, a frequent occurrence!

. . .

What's the Best Way to Get Out of Bed?

DON'T BE SURPRISED when one day you find that it has become difficult to get out of bed in the morning. You may have a hard time because you are ungainly or because you are experiencing back pain. The easiest way to get out of bed is to roll onto your side so that you are facing the side of the bed. Tip or swing your legs over the side of the bed, feet first. Once your feet touch the floor, push yourself up with your arms into a sitting position. At that point, stand up. And, of course, feel free to ask for help from your partner, especially in those last few weeks when it becomes impossible to see your feet, let alone get up out of a chair or out of bed on your own.

Another common disrupter of sleep for pregnant women is the baby! Some babies seem to get jiving right when it's bedtime. Just as you are finally settling in for a good night's sleep, it's the time that your baby decides to rev up and start kicking or squirming. This may be your baby's busiest time of the day. Even just the usual stretching of limbs and bending of elbows can keep you awake at night.

WHAT YOU CAN DO. Honestly, nothing. There is no way to settle an active baby down when you are trying to sleep. Instead, enjoy it. This is the best part of pregnancy.

Leg Cramps

If you were lucky enough to avoid leg cramps during your second trimester, you may find that you start to have them now. For other women, it's simply a continuation of what's been happening all along.

Leg cramps are quite common during the second and third trimester. These tend to occur at night, for some reason, and will wake you with a jolt. There is nothing worse than being awakened suddenly with a leg cramp. It is not completely known what causes these leg cramps, but it is believed to be the result of excess phosphorous and a shortage of calcium. Leg cramps occur in about 20 percent of women during their first trimester, and the incidence increases to 75 percent of women by the third trimester.

WHAT YOU CAN DO. There are a number of things that you can do to ward off leg cramps. First of all, spend some time at bedtime doing leg stretches. Stretching out your leg muscles before falling asleep can help avoid middle-of-the-night leg cramps. Regular exercise during the day can help, too. So if you have been becoming more and more of a couch potato, it's time to get back to getting up and going. Heavy covers can make leg cramps more likely to happen. Switch over to lighter-weight blankets that won't weigh your legs down as much and won't restrict your movements as much while you sleep. During a leg cramp, flex your foot and keep it flexed for some time. Massage and heat can help. Keep a heating pad nearby that you can quickly apply during the night when you have a leg cramp. Increase calcium and potassium in your diet. Calcium supplements can help too, but check with your doctor first before taking anything.

Can You Predict Your Baby's Sleep Patterns?

A COMMON QUESTION that pregnant women ask is whether their baby's sleep patterns in the womb predict his/her sleep schedule once born. Unfortunately, no study has ever been done to support (or refute) the belief that if a baby is most active at night, he'll be a night owl. So no one actually knows the answer to that question.

Bathroom Breaks

Bathroom breaks are back again. As your baby gets bigger, it's putting more pressure on your bladder. Your bladder is getting smaller and smaller nearly every day as your ever-growing baby compresses it.

WHAT YOU CAN DO. Similar to the first trimester, there are some things that you can do to manage these multiple trips to the bathroom throughout the night. Limit your fluid intake in the evening, being sure to keep your total amount of liquids up throughout the day. Completely empty your bladder every time you go to the bathroom. Cut out anything that increases your need to void, especially caffeine. This means cutting back on many sodas, coffee, tea, and all the other various and sundry items that have caffeine in them these days. And finally, keep lights dim when you head to the bathroom at night. Install a dimmer switch on your bathroom light or add a nightlight. The brighter the light, the more it will wake you up and thus make it harder to go right back to sleep. Instead, keep lights dim and shades pulled in your bathroom to help keep your brain in sleeping mode.

Common End-of-Pregnancy Sleep Disorders

MANY PREGNANT WOMEN develop a sleep disorder—it's very common. There are several of these sleep disturbances that can develop, including insomnia, restless legs syndrome, and snoring/sleep apnea. A brief description of each of these is provided here, with extensive explanation presented in chapter 7 (insomnia), chapter 8 (restless legs syndrome and periodic limb movement disorder), and chapter 9 (snoring and sleep apnea).

Insomnia

Having problems falling asleep or staying asleep? You are not alone! Just about every pregnant woman experiences insomnia by the end of her pregnancy. All of the issues discussed above will likely contribute to insomnia. You may have problems falling asleep at bedtime, being up several times during the night, or waking up too early in the morning and not being able to fall back to sleep. Or you could be having problems with all three!

WHAT YOU CAN DO. Chapter 7 provides all the information that you need about ways to deal with insomnia and get the sleep you need. In addition, many small changes can make all the difference.

- *If you are having problems falling asleep,* try taking a warm (not hot) bath or shower at bedtime. Try aromatherapy. A gentle massage can help, whether you give yourself a massage or have your partner give you one. There are many devices available that can be used to give yourself a massage. Put on quiet, calm music at bedtime to lull yourself to sleep. Relaxation strategies can help, too. Those strategies that they teach you in childbirth class aren't just for labor! They can help now, too.
- *Waking up in the middle of the night?* Don't just lie there tossing and turning. Get out of bed and do something quiet and soothing. Read a boring book or listen to quiet music. This is not the time to check your e-mail or turn on the national news. Write in a journal, recording your innermost thoughts for yourself and

for your baby. Having a journal of your thoughts and dreams for your developing baby can be a wonderful gift to your child.

- *And finally, getting up at 4:00 or 5:00 a.m. and can't get back to sleep?* Add room-darkening shades to your room, especially if you are pregnant during the summer months when it gets bright out much earlier. Jot down all the things that you have remembered all of a sudden that you need to get done during the day. Having a pen and notepad next to your bed can help tremendously. This will allow you to jot down all of these random thoughts without trying to figure out how in the world you are going to remember later in the day to schedule your yearly furnace cleaning and call to set up a play date for your older child.

Restless Legs Syndrome and Periodic Limb Movement Disorder

Anne knows the exact day that her sleep problems started. She was on a weekend getaway with her husband, and on their second night away she became unable to lie still at night. She had no idea what was going on, but from that point forward she was overwhelmed by the uncomfortable feelings in her legs at bedtime and throughout the entire night. She remembers pacing their hotel room all night long. Within a week of coming home, she was sleeping in their guest room because she just couldn't lie still. She felt as if she was losing her mind and wondered if she was going crazy. Neither her obstetrician nor her general doctor recognized that she had restless legs syndrome. Several years later the realization hit her after reading an article in a magazine about RLS and its effect on sleep.

Approximately 1 out of every 3 pregnant women reported symptoms consistent with restless legs syndrome (RLS). Restless legs syndrome involves intensely uncomfortable sensations in your legs that make you feel as if you need to move them. These feelings occur primarily at bedtime but also at other times that you are inactive, such as sitting for long stretches in an airplane or in a movie theater. Moving your legs helps, but only temporarily. The moment you lie still, the sensations return. As you can imagine, RLS makes it very difficult to fall asleep.

A related sleep disorder is periodic limb movement disorder (PLMD), which involves the kicking of your legs or twitching of your feet during sleep. Often RLS and PLMD occur together, but not always.

These two sleep disorders are quite prevalent during pregnancy, as they can be caused by decreased iron or folic acid, two conditions that are common to pregnancy. Iron and folic acid supplements can help a great deal, and these two conditions usually go away after childbirth. Chapter 8 presents all the information that you need about RLS and PLMD.

Snoring and Sleep Apnea

> "My husband has completely stopped sleeping with me; he sleeps on the futon. Not because he doesn't love me, but because I am a snoring machine. Like sounds that you have never heard. Of course, I never hear them, since I'm sleeping. It drives him nuts and it's clearly related to my pregnancy."
> —*Tara, 37 weeks pregnant*

Snoring is very common: between 25 and 30 percent of women report snoring during pregnancy. There are several reasons for this increase in snoring, including nasal congestion, your uterus pressing on your diaphragm, and overall weight gain.

Sleep apnea is a more serious condition that involves stopping breathing for a brief time while you are asleep. Your brain will always wake you up enough for you to start breathing. However, sleep apnea can lead to decreased oxygen in your system and to multiple arousals during the night. These arousals, which can be in the hundreds, will disrupt your sleep throughout the night and make you feel lousy the next day.

Sleeping in Separate Rooms

OFTEN BY THE end of pregnancy couples are sleeping in separate rooms. This sleeping situation is very common, although no one knows exact statistics. Whether it's because you are tossing and turning, getting up a gazillion times to use the bathroom, or have taken over the bed with your multiple pillows, don't be surprised if your bed partner has headed to another part of the house to get some sleep. There is no reason to be embarrassed or think this is wrong. In this case, it's all about sleep; everyone trying to get as much as they can.

There is a relationship between snoring/sleep apnea and other medical complications, including preeclampsia (a progressive condition characterized by high blood pressure and the presence of protein in the urine) and increased blood pressure, which can affect your baby's growth. These additional complications are rare, but it's important that they do not get missed. If you snore or are having problems breathing at night, see chapter 9, which provides complete information on these two issues. Also, be sure to speak to your doctor.

Bed Rest

Suzanne was pregnant with her third child. She had had no problems with her previous pregnancies, so she was shocked when she began having labor pains at 32 weeks. Her doctor wasn't initially concerned, but when the labor pains continued, he strongly recommended bed rest. She was allowed up to take a shower every day and to transfer from her bed to the living room couch. It was extremely difficult being on bed rest with a 3-year-old and a 5-year-old at home. Luckily, neighbors pitched in with meals, and Suzanne's mother came to stay for the last two weeks before the baby arrived.

ENDING UP ON bed rest is quite common during pregnancy. Estimates indicate that about 1 in 5 pregnant women will spend some time on bed rest. This amounts to about 750,000 women every year. Realize that if you are one of these women, you are definitely not alone.

There are many reasons your doctor might prescribe bed rest, including risk of premature labor, preeclampsia, a weak cervix, or having a preexisting medical condition, such as heart disease. When on bed rest, your entire body rests. Your heart, kidneys, and other organs do not have to work as hard. Also, the baby is not placing pressure on your cervix, thus reducing the risk of premature labor.

When you're not going through it, the idea of bed rest sounds glorious. It almost sounds like a vacation—nothing to do but lie in bed all day! You can read trashy novels, surf the Internet, and watch television to your heart's content! However, the reality of it is quite different. First of all, bed rest often implies that there is something that is not going perfectly during your pregnancy, resulting in lots of anxiety. Second, lying around all day gets old fast. There are only so many daytime television shows that you can watch. There may be concerns about your job and about caring for other children, which you hadn't anticipated happening so soon. Everyone knows that things are going to be quite different after the baby arrives, but you likely didn't expect those changes to occur while you were pregnant.

Effects of Bed Rest

Being told that you have to go on bed rest, whether at home or in the hospital, is a difficult thing. Being informed all of a sudden that you need to head right to the hospital or go home and not get out of bed will lead to lots of anxiety, including concerns about your baby and about what is going to happen in your life. Beyond the obvious, there are many effects of bed rest, spanning the physical complications, emotional responses, and impact on your family.

PHYSICAL COMPLICATIONS. As you can well imagine, the muscles in your body can easily get weak while you are on bed rest. Pregnant women who are on complete bed rest typically gain less weight, with many women actually losing weight, given their decreased appetite, neither one a situation that is best for your developing baby. You may experience other problems as a result of bed rest, including heartburn, reflux, and constipation. Women who are on complete bed rest (meaning not allowed out of bed at all) are more likely to have these complications than those who are on partial bed rest (only part of the day or never on complete bed rest for two or more days in succession).

EMOTIONAL RESPONSES. The emotional aspect of being on bed rest can be the hardest part. You are likely feeling depressed, angry, isolated, guilty, and bored. The lack of control can be the most difficult part. Being on bed rest is very stressful (nope, it's not a picnic!). You are likely highly concerned about your baby, impatient, uncertain about what is going to happen, and not happy about being put in the position of being "sick" when you probably feel perfectly fine. You are also likely to feel bored and to feel that you are missing out.

FAMILY STRESS. Bed rest can be hard on the entire family. All of a sudden you cannot care for your other children or do all the things that you normally do in a day to take care of your family and your home. If you are hospitalized, it is even harder. Being on bed rest, whether at home or at the hospital, will lead to your needing an incredible amount of help from everyone else in your household.

Don't be surprised if being on bed rest (through no fault of your own!) can be stressful on your marriage. With both of you tense and worried, you are more likely to argue and feel less supported. Fathers will find it very stressful having their wife (or partner) on bed rest, whether she is at home or at the hospital. This stress is compounded if there are other children in the household. Dads find that "doing it all" is the hardest part—managing their job, household responsibilities, and child care. In addition, fathers worry greatly about the health and well-being of their wives and their unborn baby. They are just as afraid and worried, and feel helpless to do anything to rectify the situation.

Not only is bed rest stressful for your husband/partner, it can also be very hard on your other children. Young children will have a difficult time understanding why you are not allowed to get out of bed and can't play as usual. If you are in the hospital, it's even scarier for little ones. On top of that, your children will likely feel the effects of changes with regard to who is taking care of them and all the things that usually make their lives similar from day to day.

Elena was 30 weeks pregnant and went into early labor. Her doctor immediately admitted her to the hospital. Elena's 6-year-old daughter, Hannah, had a very hard time with her mom not being home. It wasn't the big things, but the little things. Her dad wasn't able to do her hair the way her mom did, he didn't sing her usual bedtime song the "right way," and he didn't know which days she was supposed to wear sneakers to school.

FINANCIAL HARDSHIP. Being on bed rest also can be financially difficult, especially as the result of lost wages. You may not have adequate sick time or disability to cover the time that you are on bed rest. This may be particularly stressful if you were saving your sick days to take time off from work after the baby arrived. Even the little things, like your husband paying for parking to visit you in the hospital and your family relying on take-out meals, can add up quickly. One study found that 71 percent of families had problems financially as the result of bed rest, including loss of income, lost jobs, increased debt, and out-of-pocket expenses.

Sleep and Bed Rest

Not surprisingly, when you are on bed rest it is way too easy to nap during the day, so most women end up with their sleep-wake rhythm disrupted. That is, they end up sleeping throughout the day and then are often awake during the night. The vicious cycle continues with sleeping during the day followed by restless nights. Stick to your usual schedule as much as you can. Go to "bed" at your usual time and continue to get up in the morning at your normal wake time. If you nap, make it a short nap in the early afternoon.

You may also find that you are more tired while on bed rest. How can that be? All that you are doing all day is lying around. However, doing nothing is tiring in and of itself. It also can be incredibly boring and tedious.

Questions to Ask Your Health Care Provider

IF YOU HAVE been told that you need to go on bed rest, ask your health care provider lots of questions, so that you can be sure to take care of yourself and your developing baby.

- **DO I NEED TO STAY IN BED ALL DAY?** Be sure to ask what exactly your doctor means by "bed rest." Do you need to be in bed all day, most of the day, or just a few hours each day? Some women are put on total bed rest, whereas other women just need to rest for several hours a day.

- **DO I HAVE TO LIE IN A CERTAIN POSITION?** Some women need to lie in a specific position, such as on their side or with their feet propped up. Ask your doctor what is recommended. Can you spend much of the day sitting up, or do you need to literally be lying down?

- **WHAT ACTIVITIES CAN I SAFELY DO?** Ask what you are allowed to do and what you are not allowed to do. Are you allowed to get up and shower? Can you make trips to the bathroom? Can you get up and tuck in your 3-year-old at bedtime? Can you pick up your toddler? For some women, it's okay to cook a meal or do your child's bedtime routine. Other women can continue working but need to lie down when they are at home. And even others are required to literally stay in bed, with sponge baths and bedpans.

- **CAN I EXERCISE?** Ask your doctor whether you can safely do any exercises. Exercise can be helpful to keep your muscles toned and loose. Some exercises that may be safe for you to do include Kegel exercise (muscle exercises that tighten the pelvic area), deep breathing, pelvic tilts, neck circles, and even leg lifts. But be sure to ask before you attempt any of these exercises.
- **WHAT SHOULD I DO TO AVOID OTHER PROBLEMS?** Ask your health care provider what you can do to avoid bedsores, backaches, and blood clots that can occur as the result of lying in one spot all the time.

Surviving Bed Rest

Below is a list of things that you can do to manage being on bed rest and keep your sanity.

- **FIND SUPPORT.** There are some extremely helpful websites focused on bed rest. Connecting with other women who are also on bed rest can help tremendously. You can share tips on how to survive, and it's nice to be in touch with others who are going through the exact same thing. One such website is Sidelines.org.
- **MOVIE AND BOOKS-ON-TAPE RENTALS.** Subscribing to a plan like Netflix can be a sanity saver. Rent several movies at a time. It's the perfect time to catch up on the classics and the newest movies that you missed. Comehearbooks.com delivers books on tape through

the mail. You can also download books from iTunes or
Audible.com. So whether it's the most recent novel or
an old classic like *Jane Eyre*, you can catch up on your
"reading."

- **KEEP ENTERTAINED.** In addition to movies and books on
  tape, have someone get you a basketful of magazines to
  read. Ask friends for a list of their favorite books. This
  may not be the time you want to tackle *War and Peace*, or
  maybe it is. Be sure the television remote control is nearby (this may be the time you subscribe to all those extra
  cable channels). A laptop with a wireless connection can
  help you stay connected to friends and family through e-
  mail and instant messaging. Other good activities include
  knitting or doing needlepoint. Making something for the
  baby's room can keep you focused and motivated.

- **PAMPER YOURSELF.** There is nothing like a pregnancy
  massage, a manicure, a pedicure, or a facial when
  you're home in bed. Many places will send someone
  out to your home to pamper you. If you can't afford a
  professional manicure or pedicure, invite your favorite
  gal friends over, and everyone can enjoy themselves
  painting their toenails and indulging in a mud mask.

- **GET COMFORTABLE.** Make wherever you're going to be
  on bed rest a haven. Indulge in comfy pajamas and
  a decadent fleece blanket or down comforter. Have
  everything that you need easily accessible. Get a basket and fill it with crossword puzzle books, a favorite
  novel, the remote control, a cordless phone, and some
  snacks. Keep this basket within easy reach.

- **ACCEPT HELP.** If you are on bed rest, you can't do it on
  your own. You are going to need help. Hire a service
  that delivers meals, comes and cleans your house, or

mows your lawn. You can hire a local teen to walk your dog.

- **EAT HEALTHILY.** As much as it may sound wonderful to stock up on junk food and desserts, be sure to eat nutritious foods and drink plenty of fluids. Healthy foods will help you feel better and are best for your developing baby. Also, eating junk food can lead to extra pounds that are bad for your and your baby's health, and means more to lose after the baby is born. Keep on hand a basket of snacks that includes healthy items, such as fruit and cereal bars. They may not be as fun as a chocolate bar or a bag of potato chips, but you'll be better off for it in the long run.

- **KEEP A SCHEDULE.** Even if it seems that you have all day, keeping a daily schedule can be a sanity saver. Schedule time for meals so that you're not just snacking all day. Some women find that it helps to get "dressed" for daytime and change into pajamas when it's "bedtime."

- **RELAX.** And most important, relax! The whole reason that you are on bed rest is to relax, so feel free to while away the hours daydreaming and relaxing. Try not to get too stressed about all the things that you can't do. Instead, realize that staying in bed is the most important thing that you can be doing at the moment to take care of your baby.

Looking Ahead

HOW YOU ARE sleeping in the last month or two of your pregnancy can be a glimpse into your future. How much and how well you sleep during pregnancy can be an indication of how long your labor will last, your risk of having a cesarean section, and whether you may develop postpartum depression.

> ### Bed Rest in the Hospital
>
> **IF YOU HAVE** been hospitalized, bed rest can be even harder. There are some basic things that you can do to help make your stay in the hospital more comfortable. Bring your own nightgown/pajamas and your own toiletries. Put a picture of your kids or your husband on your nightstand. Most hospitals let you use your own pillow and blankets. Splurge on your own sheets if you are going to be in the hospital for a while. Have lots of distractions available, such as books, magazines, playing cards, and puzzles. See if you can bring a laptop with you and set up an Internet connection. Have a weekly "date night" with your husband. He can bring take-out from your favorite restaurant, and a movie.

Sleep and Labor

Amazingly, there seems to be a connection between how much sleep a woman gets and how long she is in labor. A recent study found that women who slept less than 6 hours a night three weeks before they were due had longer labors and were much more likely to need a cesarean section. Those women who were getting less than 6 hours of sleep at night were in labor for an average of 29 hours and their chance of having a C-section was 37 percent. This was in contrast to those women who were getting 7 or more hours of sleep, who were in labor for about 18 hours, and whose C-section rate was only 11 percent. Not a bad trade-off—one extra hour of sleep every night for 10 hours less in labor!

Sleep Patterns and Postpartum Depression

How you are sleeping at the end of your pregnancy can also be predictive of postpartum depression. Research has shown that women whose sleep is highly disrupted at the end of their pregnancy are more likely to feel depressed several months later.

Those women whose sleep is the most problematic at the end of pregnancy are also much more likely to develop postpartum depression. So if you are having a hard time sleeping at the end of your pregnancy, be sure to watch for signs of postpartum depression and get help right away. In addition, see chapter 10 to plan ahead for ways to reduce the likelihood of developing postpartum depression.

And Finally . . . Learn About Infant Sleep Now

Now is the time to start learning about infant sleep and ways that you can help your baby become a great sleeper at a young age. Chapter 12 is a good place to start and will give you much of the information that you need. In addition, read some books about infant sleep. Once your baby is born, you will have much less time to read, and being sleep-deprived yourself, you will have a harder time making logical, well-thought-out decisions. It is much better to be prepared now and have a strategy in mind. Many studies show that educating soon-to-be or new moms about their babies' sleep habits makes a huge difference. These families' babies end up being much better sleepers, even by 3 months of age.

Third Trimester Sleep Tips

- **KEEP SLEEP A PRIORITY.** Get plenty of rest and keep getting 8 hours of sleep.
- **SLEEP ON YOUR LEFT SIDE.** It's best to sleep on your left side and avoid lying on your back for long periods. Sleeping on your left side allows for the best flow of blood to your baby.
- **KEEP EXERCISING.** Although it may be getting harder to exercise, it will help you sleep better at night and help you feel your best during the day.
- **AVOID CAFFEINE.** Check out what you are drinking to be sure that there are no surprises. Many drinks unexpectedly contain caffeine.
- **CHECK OUT SNORING.** If you are snoring at night, let your health care provider know so that you can be evaluated for preeclampsia.
- **CHECK YOUR IRON.** If you are having symptoms of restless legs syndrome, have your iron and folic acid levels checked.
- **WARD OFF LEG CRAMPS.** Get plenty of calcium and potassium in your diet to ward off leg cramps. If you do have a cramp during the night, flex your foot upward. Do a few of these calf stretches before you go to bed at night, too.

Reminders

- Almost all women have some difficulties sleeping during the third trimester, especially with problems falling asleep and waking at night. Being sleepy during the day is also common.

- It's time to return to going to bed early if you switched back to your prepregnancy schedule during the second trimester.
- Ease heartburn by eating smaller meals, eating slowly, avoiding certain foods, and drinking plenty of fluids.
- It's definitely time to work on finding a comfortable sleeping position. Try using lots of pillows or a body pillow. Some women find it easier to sleep in a recliner chair.
- There is not much that you can do about your baby's kicking keeping you awake at night. Don't get frustrated; instead, enjoy it. This is one of the best parts of pregnancy.
- Snoring and sleep apnea frequently develop during the third trimester, as does restless legs syndrome. Be sure and talk to your health care provider.
- About 20 percent of pregnant women end up on bed rest. Bed rest can be difficult on you emotionally, physically, and financially. Come up with a strategy to help you survive bed rest.
- Get plenty of sleep during your last trimester, as sleep is linked to shorter labor and less chance of a cesarean section.
- Learn about infant sleep now so that you can help your baby become a great sleeper.

PART III

Solving Common
Sleep Problems

SEVEN

Insomnia

> "I fall asleep fine, but then I'm awake almost every night between 2:30 and 5:00 in the morning. I feel crummy during the day since I'm so exhausted from not sleeping. Every day I worry that I'm not going to be able to sleep that night."
>
> —*Gina, 14 weeks pregnant*

> "Although the baby is now sleeping through the night, I still wake up several times."
>
> —*Katie, new mom to 4-month-old Grace*

We've all experienced those early-morning hours spent lying wide-awake in bed, watching the minutes on the clock tick past, thinking about everything that needs to be accomplished the following day, and feeling desperate to fall back asleep. Insomnia strikes most women at some time in their lives but can be more intense during pregnancy. During pregnancy, women are more likely to have problems both falling asleep and staying asleep. Once the baby arrives, new moms typically do not have problems falling asleep; rather; they have more difficulties with waking up during the night. Insomnia involves difficulty initiating or maintaining sleep—that is, problems falling asleep at bedtime or waking up during the night. The sleeplessness that results from insomnia is extremely frustrating and leaves most women irritable and fatigued the next day.

In the general population, studies indicate that approximately 30 to 40 percent of adults have experienced some insomnia symptoms over the past year, and 10 to 15 percent of adults have chronic insomnia. Insomnia is twice as common for women than men. During pregnancy, the prevalence of insomnia increases, affecting up to 80 percent of expecting women. Insomnia is less common after the baby is born compared to pregnancy, but women still continue to have difficulties with middle-of-the-night awakenings.

Symptoms of Insomnia

THERE ARE TWO primary symptoms of insomnia.

1. **DIFFICULTY SLEEPING.** Women with insomnia have problems sleeping, whether it is falling asleep at night, waking in the middle of the night, or waking up too early in the morning and not being able to return to sleep.

2. **DAYTIME IMPAIRMENT.** To be classified as insomnia, having difficulty sleeping at night needs to lead to some level of daytime impairment, whether at home, on the job, or socially. Possible indications of daytime impairment can include any of the following:

   - **FATIGUE OR SLEEPINESS.** Insomnia can lead to feeling tired or sleepy the next day. You may end up being lethargic or even having to take a nap because you didn't sleep well the night before.
   - **LACK OF ENERGY OR MOTIVATION.** You may not have the energy to get things done.
   - **DECREASED ATTENTION AND CONCENTRATION.** As a result of the sleep deprivation caused by insomnia, some people will have problems with concentration

at work or at school, especially when listening to a lecture or in a meeting.

- **MEMORY IMPAIRMENT.** You may have difficulty remembering things if you didn't sleep well the night before.
- **EFFECTS ON MOOD.** Many people with insomnia feel depressed or anxious. You may be irritable and have little energy.
- **ERRORS OR ACCIDENTS.** As a result of sleeplessness, you may make mistakes that you normally wouldn't while at work or when driving.
- **HEADACHES, GASTROINTESTINAL PROBLEMS, OR OTHER PHYSICAL SYMPTOMS.** Not getting enough sleep can result in physical symptoms such as headaches or stomach distress.
- **CONCERNS OR WORRIES ABOUT SLEEP.** People with insomnia often worry about their lack of sleep and worry during the day about whether they will be able to sleep that night.

Quiz

Do You Have Insomnia?

ANSWER THE QUESTIONS below from the Insomnia Severity Index questionnaire to figure out whether you have insomnia and how severe it may be.

Q1. Please rate the current (last 2 weeks) SEVERITY of your insomnia problem(s)

	None	Mild	Moderate	Very severe	Severe
Difficulty falling asleep	0	1	2	3	4
Difficulty staying asleep	0	1	2	3	4
Problem waking up too early	0	1	2	3	4

Q2. How SATISFIED/dissatisfied are you with your current sleep pattern?

Very satisfied				Very dissatisfied
0	1	2	3	4

Q3. To what extent do you consider your sleep problem to INTERFERE with your daily functioning (e.g., daytime fatigue, ability to function at work/daily chores, concentration, memory, mood, etc)?

Not at all interfering	A little	Somewhat	Much	Very much interfering
0	1	2	3	4

Q4. How WORRIED/distressed are you about your current sleep problem?

Not at all	A little	Somewhat	Much	Very much
0	1	2	3	4

SCORING. Add up your scores for all of the items. Scores range from 0 to 28.

What does your score mean?

SCORE	
0 to 7	No significant insomnia
8 to 14	Mild insomnia
15 to 21	Moderate insomnia
22 to 28	Severe insomnia

What Causes Insomnia?

Paula has a 15-month-old son and is 5 months pregnant. She thought that being pregnant and keeping up with a toddler all day would leave her so exhausted that she would crash at night. However, on most nights, her mind starts racing the moment she crawls into bed and it could be hours until she finally falls asleep.

INSOMNIA CAN HAVE many triggers, which makes it different from the other sleep disorders discussed in chapters 8 and 9. It is important to understand that not all women who have problems sleeping actually have insomnia. Many other sleep disorders, such as sleep apnea and restless legs syndrome, interfere with a woman's ability to fall asleep, and thus are experienced as insomnia, but they really aren't insomnia in the pure sense of the term. If those underlying conditions are alleviated, the insomnia symptom goes away.

Some women have insomnia as the result of anxiety or depression. However, most women's insomnia is learned. Something happens that interferes with your sleep, like pregnancy or the birth of a baby. Once sleep becomes disturbed, it continues to be problematic, because there is an association between not being able to sleep and situations and behaviors that are associated with sleep, such as lying in bed. Then lying in bed, where you just spent several sleepless nights, will cause you to feel tense and frustrated. These feelings will make it even more difficult for you to fall asleep. Once the pattern is established, it can continue for days, weeks, or months.

Often insomniacs develop poor sleep habits to combat the sleep problems, such as spending too much time in bed, not keeping to a consistent bedtime and wake time, and napping during the day. Although a short nap early in the day can be a good idea if you're tired, if you have insomnia, napping is likely to interfere with your nighttime sleep.

Insomniacs also experience a "racing mind" of negative thoughts, including anxious thoughts about being unable to fall asleep. This leads to a vicious cycle: the more you try to fall asleep and think, "I'll never be able to sleep tonight," the more agitated you become, and the less likely you will be to fall asleep.

Causes of Insomnia During Pregnancy

Insomnia is especially likely when you are pregnant. Here are just some of the possible reasons—there are more, but these are the most common.

- Discomfort due to the increasing size of your belly
- Back pain
- Heartburn
- Frequent urination during the night
- Anxiety
- Anticipating the arrival of your baby
- Hormonal changes
- Leg cramps

Are Anxious Thoughts Keeping You Up at Night?

A PRIMARY REASON for having problems sleeping is that you are lying in bed with your mind on high alert. Worrying is a surefire way to keep you up all night. Unfortunately, it is much too easy to worry when you are pregnant. Think of all the things that are so easy to worry about during pregnancy (I'm sure that all of these have already crossed your mind):

- Is the baby going to be okay?
- Can I/we afford this baby?
- Will I love this baby as much as I love my older child(ren)?
- Is the baby going to be okay? (Back to thinking about this again!)

- How am I ever going to able to juggle working with being a mom?
- How and when do I tell my boss that I am pregnant?
- I wonder if the baby is going to cause problems with my relationship with my partner?

And I'm sure that you can come up with a gazillion more things to worry about while pregnant.

WHAT YOU CAN DO. It's hard to control worrying once you get started; however, there are ways to manage worrying.

- **SHARE YOUR THOUGHTS.** The best way to get control of your worrying is to share your thoughts. Talk to your partner. He's probably having similar thoughts. Call your best friend or your sister. Check in with another mom-to-be. She's definitely going to understand your concerns. If you don't know anyone who is pregnant, there are many online support communities of other moms-to-be.
- **WRITE DOWN YOUR THOUGHTS.** Journaling can be a great anxiety reliever. It lets you record your thoughts, your worries, and your anxieties, all without having to filter them for the benefit of others. This technique can help in the middle of the night when your thoughts are racing. Writing them down can help ease your mind.
- **STOP YOUR THOUGHTS.** As impossible as it may sound, you actually can stop yourself from worrying. Every time you start to worry, stop yourself and think of something else. With practice, you'll get much better at not drifting immediately back to worrying.
- **TALK TO YOUR DOCTOR ABOUT PREGNANCY-RELATED WORRIES.** If you are worried about something specific related to your pregnancy or your developing baby,

talk to your health care practitioner. Your practitioner can talk to you about your concerns, and even do an ultrasound to check out the status of your baby.

● **DON'T WORRY ABOUT SLEEP.** And finally, try not to worry about not being able to sleep, although that is easier said than done. The more you worry about it, the worse the problem will get, making it harder for you to fall asleep and making you feel worse during the day.

Getting Sleep: What You Can Do

THE BEST WAY to solve insomnia depends on what is causing the problem. For example, is the insomnia new to your pregnancy? Is it a continuing problem? If it's related to depression or anxiety, then the best treatment is psychotherapy or medication. Another possible cause is that it really is due to another sleep disorder, such as sleep apnea or restless legs syndrome. If this is the case, treating the actual sleep disorder will cure the problem.

If your insomnia is not caused by depression, anxiety, or another sleep disorder but involves some other disturbance of your normal sleep routine, there are two primary options: general sleep strategies that can be very effective and behavioral treatments that are specific for insomnia.

Sleep Strategies

There are many things that you can do to help you sleep better at night when you are dealing with insomnia. Below are some simple changes that you can make.

WARM BATH. A warm bath or shower as part of your bedtime routine can often help. The warmth of the bath or shower will affect your body temperature, which helps you to feel tired and prolongs deeper natural sleep. Be careful not to take too hot a bath or shower, though, while you are pregnant.

MASSAGE. A massage can be a wonderful way to relax and get sleepy. A willing partner does wonders. Otherwise, feel free to give yourself a massage. Even just a foot massage is a great way to erase the stresses of the day.

AROMATHERAPY. Some women find that using aromatherapy can be very relaxing. You can add scented oils to your bath, light scented candles, or use scented lotions. Using the same scent every single night at bedtime can help you associate that smell with sleep.

PLAY RELAXING MUSIC OR SOUNDS. Some women find that playing soothing background music or other kinds of sounds (think ocean or rainfall) can help them relax and settle down to a good night's sleep.

KEEP A STRICT SLEEP SCHEDULE. It is best to maintain a strict sleep schedule in which you go to bed at the same time every night and wake up at the same time every morning. Going to bed and waking up at the same time every day sets your internal clock, helping you to fall asleep at bedtime and wake up in the morning. Setting your internal clock so that you are sleepy at the same time every night will make it easier for you to fall asleep.

DON'T STAY IN BED TOO LONG. Often women with insomnia stay in bed too long. Don't stay in bed for nine or ten hours if you need only eight hours of sleep. It is better to be in bed only the exact number of hours that you need to sleep. Staying in bed for just the hours that you need will consolidate your sleep, especially if you have long periods of being awake in the middle of the night or if you wake too early in the morning.

ELIMINATE ALCOHOL. If you are pregnant, hopefully you are not drinking alcohol, but you should know that alcohol will interfere with your sleep. Eliminating alcohol can combat middle-of-the night and early morning awakenings.

DON'T WATCH THE CLOCK. For many women, staring at the clock and watching every minute creep by makes them more and more anxious. Again, worrying about not sleeping will only make the problem worse. Remind yourself that there is also never good news when you look at the clock during the night. If you've been lying awake for a long time and the clock tells you that you've been lying there for over an hour, that's bad news. If you wake up and it's 3:00 a.m., that's also bad news. And if you wake up and see that it's 5:00 in the morning and you're dreading having to get up at 6:00, again it's bad news. For most, staring at the time will simply make you feel worse, so turn your clock to the wall and no peeking!

OR WATCH THE CLOCK AND STAY UP AS LONG AS POSSIBLE. On the other hand, some insomniac women find that simply watching the clock and trying to stay awake as long as possible helps. Do this for a few nights in a row, and you will learn that you can still function the next day with less sleep than you prefer—decreasing how much you worry when you can't fall asleep on other nights. This suggestion, while it seems to counter all the other advice provided in this book, can be helpful for some, but it may not work for all.

SLEEP IN ANOTHER ROOM FOR A FEW NIGHTS. Some women find that they sleep much better if they make a change, such as sleeping in another room in their house. If you have a spare bedroom, try sleeping there for a few nights. Often your bedroom becomes associated with not sleeping, so making a mental shift can do wonders.

EXERCISE DURING THE DAY. Exercising during the day can help you sleep at night. It is best to exercise at least a few hours before bedtime.

TURN OFF THE ELECTRONICS. Turn off the e-mail, the instant messaging, and the television. Even better, get all of these sleep-busting gadgets out of your bedroom! All of these things are going to be highly stimulating and make it hard for you to turn your brain off. Checking your e-mail right before bed is probably the worst culprit, as there is always a chance of reading something that is upsetting, and there is little that you can do about it late at night.

MAKE YOUR BEDROOM SLEEP CONDUCIVE. Be sure that your bedroom is set to help you get a good night's sleep. It should be dark, cool, quiet, and comfortable. Get room-darkening shades or heavy curtains. Set the temperature in your bedroom so it's comfortable. A white-noise machine or just a noisy fan can block out noise, helping you to sleep. And finally, make your bed and bedroom a sleep haven, with wonderful bedding, comfy pillows, and a soothing atmosphere.

DEVELOP A BEDTIME ROUTINE. Just as you will soon be developing a bedtime routine for your baby, you need one, too. Have a relaxing bedtime routine for yourself that you do every night, such as a warm shower, massaging yourself with lotion, and reading a favorite book.

PRACTICE GOOD SLEEP HABITS. Keep good sleep habits. Chapter 3 provides a list of the best do's and don'ts for getting a good night's sleep. Follow all of them to help you sleep at night.

Tuning Out the World

LIGHT AND NOISE can make it very hard to sleep, especially if you are a light sleeper. To help you sleep, you can try some of the following to keep the world at bay. If you have kids, though, you will need to be sure that you can hear them so that you can respond to them during the night. Even better, if you have a partner, get some sleep yourself and have him or her be on kid duty.

- **BLOCK OUT THE NOISE.** Any kind of constant noise will help mask noise, whether it is coming from within your household (someone getting up early in the morning) or from outside (such as passing traffic, barking dogs, or noisy neighbors). A noisy fan will do the trick, as will setting a radio to the end of the dial. More expensive sound machines will also work. On many of these, you can choose from a multitude of background noises, such as the sound of rain, a babbling brook, ocean waves, crickets, or wind chimes. Any of these sounds will help you tune out distracting noises.
- **EARPLUGS.** Try earplugs if you are really sensitive to noise. There are many kinds of earplugs, so try several different kinds to find the one that is most comfortable for you.
- **BLOCK OUT THE LIGHT.** Dark curtains will help block out morning light (or light from the street or neighborhood); room-darkening shades are even better. Some women even find that eyeshades or eye pillows (a small rectangle pillow that goes over the eyes) do the trick (think Greta Garbo). These may help you fall asleep and sleep later in the morning, especially in the summer, when the sun rises so early in the morning.

Behavioral Strategies

THERE HAS BEEN a great deal of research on behavioral strategies to treat insomnia. A recent National Institutes of Health (NIH) state-of-the-science consensus statement concluded that behavioral treatments are as effective as prescription medications for short-term treatment of insomnia and likely more effective in the long term.

Relaxation

Relaxation is an excellent strategy that can help you fall asleep at night. Research has shown that relaxation training is effective in 45 percent of people with insomnia. Relaxation strategies can also be helpful in stressful situations.

You can learn to relax using a number of different strategies, including progressive muscle relaxation, guided imagery, and meditation. Try out a few and decide what works best to help you fall asleep. There are also books available to teach you ways to relax.

PROGRESSIVE MUSCLE RELAXATION. Progressive muscle relaxation (PMR) is the gold standard of relaxation strategies. It takes practice, but once learned it is an excellent way to reduce stress and help you relax. Progressive muscle relaxation teaches you to identify and relieve tension in your muscles.

To practice PMR, tense and relax each muscle in sequence. In the beginning, progressive muscle relaxation takes between twenty and thirty minutes. The more you practice, the less time it will take. Eventually, you will be able to relax in a matter of moments.

Follow the script outlined below. You can record an audio version of it to listen to as you rest. However, if you are like many people who don't like to hear the sound of your own voice, get someone else to do this for you. The person should speak in a slow, soothing manner. The exact words used don't matter, as long as they cover the process. You don't even need to follow a script as long as you sequentially tense and relax your muscles. Each time that you tense a muscle, keep it tensed for about ten seconds.

Progressive Muscle Relaxation Script

MUSCLE GROUP	TENSING EXERCISE
Lower arms	Make a fist
Upper arms	Make a muscle
Lower legs	Point toes
Thighs	Squeeze legs together
Stomach	Tighten stomach muscles
Chest	Take a deep breath
Shoulders	Raise shoulders to ears
Neck	Lower chin to chest
Jaw	Bite down firmly
Lips	Press lips together
Eyes	Close eyes tightly
Forehead	Frown, draw eyebrows together

To begin this exercise, find a comfortable position, perhaps lying on a bed or sitting in a reclining chair. Remove your glasses (if you wear them), get comfortable, and close your eyes. Keep your eyes closed throughout the relaxation process.

Start by taking a few deep breaths. Breathe relaxation in and breathe tension out.

(Wait 20 seconds.)

Now tense the muscles of your right hand by making a fist. Feel the tension . . . study the tension . . . and relax. Notice the difference between the tension and the relaxation.

(Wait 20 seconds.)

Now tense the muscles of your right arm by making a muscle. Feel the tension . . . study the tension . . . and relax. Notice the difference.

(Wait 5 seconds.)

Just let yourself become more and more relaxed. Feel your muscles becoming loose . . . heavy . . . and relaxed. Just let your muscles go.

(Wait 5 seconds.)

Now tense the muscles of your left hand by making a fist. Feel the tension . . . study the tension . . . and relax. Notice the difference between the tension and the relaxation.

(Wait 20 seconds.)

Now tense the muscles of your left arm by making a muscle. Feel the tension . . . study the tension . . . and relax. Notice the difference.

(Wait 5 seconds.)

You are becoming more and more relaxed, sleepy and relaxed.

(Wait 5 seconds.)

Now tense the muscles of your right leg by pointing your toes. Feel the tension . . . study the tension . . . and relax. Notice the difference between the tension and the relaxation.

(Wait 20 seconds.)

Now tense the muscles of your left leg by pointing your toes. Feel the tension ... study the tension ... and relax. Notice the difference.

(Wait 5 seconds.)

Just continue to relax.

(Wait 5 seconds.)

Now tense the muscles of your upper legs by pressing your thighs together. Feel the tension ... study the tension ... and relax. Notice the difference between the tension and the relaxation.

(Wait 20 seconds.)

Now tense the muscles of your stomach. Feel the tension ... study the tension ... and relax. Notice the difference.

(Wait 5 seconds.)

The relaxation is becoming deeper and deeper. You are feeling relaxed, drowsy and relaxed. With each breath in, your relaxation increases. With each exhalation, you spread the relaxation throughout your body.

(Wait 5 seconds.)

Now tense the muscles of your chest by taking a deep breath. Feel the tension ... study the tension ... and exhale. Notice the difference between the tension and the relaxation.

(Wait 20 seconds.)

Now tense the muscles of your shoulders by hunching your shoulders toward your ears. Feel the tension ... study the tension ... and relax. Notice the difference.

(Wait 5 seconds.)

Let yourself become more and more relaxed.

(Wait 5 seconds.)

Now tense the muscles of your jaw by biting down firmly. Feel the tension . . . study the tension . . . and relax. Notice the difference between the tension and the relaxation.

(Wait 20 seconds.)

Now tense the muscles of your lower face by pressing your lips together firmly. Feel the tension . . . study the tension . . . and relax. Notice the difference.

(Wait 5 seconds.)

Now the very deep state of relaxation is moving through all the areas of your body as your muscles completely relax.

(Wait 5 seconds.)

Now tense the muscles of your eyes by closing them tightly. Feel the tension . . . study the tension . . . and exhale. Notice the difference between the tension and the relaxation.

(Wait 20 seconds.)

Now tense the muscles of your forehead by frowning and drawing your eyebrows together. Feel the tension . . . study the tension . . . and relax. Notice the difference.

(Wait 5 seconds.)

Let yourself become more and more relaxed.

(Wait 20 seconds.)

Now relax all the muscles of your body; just let them become more and more relaxed.

(Wait 20 seconds.)

Remain in your very relaxed state. Begin to notice your breathing. Breathe through your nose. Notice the cool air as you breathe in and the warm moist air as you exhale. Just continue to notice your breathing. Now each time you exhale, mentally repeat the word *relax*. Inhale, exhale, relax . . . inhale, exhale, relax.

(Wait 20 seconds.)

Now you are going to return to your normal, alert state. As I count backward, you will gradually become more alert. When I reach "two," open your eyes. When I get to "one," you will be entirely alert. "Five . . . four" . . . you are becoming more alert . . ."three" . . . you feel very refreshed . . ."two" . . . now open your eyes . . ."one."

You should feel extremely relaxed after doing PMR. Continue to practice. That is the only way to get good at this technique. Even if you feel completely relaxed after the first time, you will feel more and more relaxed each time you practice. After a number of sessions (over at least one or two weeks), cut back the number of muscle groups by half (tense and relax both fists together, both arms together, both legs together, then the thighs, chest, neck, lips, eyes). Practice again for one or two weeks. Cut back the muscle groups again by half (both arms, both legs, chest, lips). By now you should be an expert at becoming relaxed. Once you are good at PMR, the word *relax* will be well associated with a completely relaxed state. Use the word *relax* in your everyday life to help you relax in tense situations, and especially at bedtime to help you fall asleep.

DIAPHRAGMATIC BREATHING. Slow, even breathing is another excellent way to relax. Many people breathe shallowly from their upper chest. This type of breathing can cause you to hyperventilate. A better way to breathe is from your diaphragm. This technique will take only a few moments to learn. A warning, though—this technique is easier to learn earlier in your pregnancy, before your belly is completely bulging.

First, lie down on your back on the floor or on a bed. Place your hand on your chest and breathe using your chest muscles so that you feel your chest rise and fall with each breath. Keeping that hand on your chest, place your other hand on your stomach. Continue to breathe from your chest noticing that your stomach muscles hardly move. Now breathe from your diaphragm. This will require you to take deeper breaths. When you breathe from your diaphragm, your chest will hardly move and your stomach will rise and fall. Continue doing this for a few minutes and get the feel of it. Once you think you have it, sit up, leaving your hands in place on your chest and stomach. Continue to practice diaphragmatic breathing—that is, breathing from your diaphragm. When you are ready, stand up and continue to breathe from your diaphragm. Again, keep your hands where they are while you get the hang of it. If you think you have lost the feeling for the process, return to a lying position.

When you first use this technique, you will need to place your hand on your stomach to make sure that you are breathing from your diaphragm. As you get better at it, you will no longer need to do this. When doing diaphragmatic breathing, take slow, deep breaths. Don't breathe too fast, or you may hyperventilate, which will make you feel even more stressed. Take several deep breaths. Then breathe normally. Take several deep breaths again. Within a few minutes you should feel calmer and more relaxed.

Diaphragmatic breathing is an excellent stress reducer in any situation, not just at bedtime to help you fall asleep. If you are about to give a presentation and are feeling stressed, do your diaphragmatic breathing. Upset with your spouse and feeling stressed? Do a few minutes of deep breathing. This type of deep breathing can be done anywhere. No one will even know that you are performing a stress relaxation technique. You can do it at home, while in a store, or out at a restaurant. Deep breathing will send messages to your body to calm down. It will change your body's reaction to stress.

GUIDED IMAGERY. Guided imagery is another excellent way to relax. At times, we all imagine ourselves to be somewhere else. If you imagine yourself in a stressful situation, such as having to make a stressful presentation or being in danger, you will become tense. Your body will react as if you are actually in that situation. Your heart will pound, your pulse will race, and you may feel jittery all over. On the other hand, if you imagine yourself in a pleasant, relaxing scene, your breathing will become more even and your pulse will slow. Imagining yourself in such a pleasant situation will help you relax.

The first thing you will need to do is develop a pleasant scenario. Lie back, close your eyes, and think of your favorite place. Maybe your relaxing place is on top of a mountain, on a beach, or in front of a fireplace. Whatever your scene, think of it using all your senses. What do you hear? What do you smell? What do you feel? The more senses that you engage, the easier it will be to imagine. Once you have developed your scene, imagine yourself there two to three times a day. Embellish it until you can actually feel yourself there. With practice you will be able to imagine yourself in your peaceful setting almost instantaneously and will quickly feel relaxed. When you are lying in bed wide awake, put yourself at your scene and enjoy the sensation.

OTHER RELAXATION STRATEGIES. There are many other ways that you can relax. You can do yoga, you can meditate.

Whatever works for you, do it. Being relaxed is as important for your mental well-being as it is to help you sleep.

Associate Your Bed with Sleep

Another well-established behavioral treatment for insomnia is called stimulus control. The basis behind stimulus control is to associate your bed only with sleep, not anything else. This means not lying in bed tossing and turning, not paying bills in bed, and not having a heated discussion with your husband in bed. Basically, you should do nothing but sleep in your bed (although romance is allowed!). All of these other behaviors that you may engage in while in your bed or bedroom can contribute to insomnia. The same holds true for resting in bed or lying in bed for a long time hoping to eventually fall asleep. The basic principles of stimulus control include the following:

- Only go to bed when you feel sleepy.
- Avoid all activities other than sleep in your bedroom (again, romance is fine).
- Sleep only in your bedroom. No falling asleep on the couch!
- Get out of bed if you are awake. If you are awake for 15 to 20 minutes, get out of bed and do something elsewhere in the house.
- Head back to bed when you are sleepy.

Sleep Restriction

Sleep restriction is another behavioral treatment for insomnia that can be very helpful. For someone with insomnia, the bed often gets associated with not sleeping, frustration, and just general tossing and turning. Instead, you want your bed to be associated only with falling asleep. This is the reason many people have no problem falling asleep on the couch in the evening, but the moment they get in bed they are wide awake and can't fall asleep. That is because their bed has become a place to toss and turn rather than sleep. To combat this association, some people find that greatly restricting their time in bed can be very helpful. Sleep restriction will help you pair your bed with sleeping instead, similar to stimulus control.

There are several steps to doing sleep restriction:

STEP ONE. Keep a sleep diary for one or two weeks to determine how much you actually sleep. By keeping a sleep diary you can calculate the average amount of time you sleep per night. A sleep diary can be found in appendix A.

STEP TWO. Figure out the average amount of time you actually sleep while you are in bed. That is, add up all of your nighttime hours of sleep and divide by 7 (one week) or 14 (two weeks).

STEP THREE. Change your sleep schedule so that you are literally in bed the amount of time that you calculated in step two. It is easier to move your bedtime later to restrict your sleep than it is to wake up earlier in the morning.

STEP FOUR. Once you are sleeping for most of the time that you are in bed, gradually increase that time by 15 minutes or so. Keep increasing the time that you are in bed by 15- to 30-minute increments once you are sleeping most of the time that you are in bed.

At first you may find that you get less sleep than usual and that you may be a bit sleepier during the day. This rarely lasts more than a few days to a week. As each day goes by, you will likely feel sleepier at bedtime, fall asleep faster, and spend less time awake during the night. Soon you will find that your bed is associated with sleep rather than tossing and turning.

Rebecca kept a sleep diary for two weeks. She found that she was going to bed at 10:30 every night but not falling asleep until midnight or later. She got up at 6:30 during the week but often slept in until 10:00 or even later on weekends, although she rarely went to bed before 1:00 or 2:00 a.m. on those nights. She averaged six and a half hours of sleep during the week and about seven hours on weekends. To start sleep restriction, she limited himself to being in bed only six and a half hours a night for one week. By the end of that week she was sleeping almost the entire time she was in bed. She then increased the amount of time that she was in bed to six hours and forty-five minutes and added fifteen minutes every few nights. It took her several weeks to get to the seven and half hours that she thought she needed. She found that she was now falling asleep much more quickly and sleeping most of the time she was in bed.

Medication

MANY PEOPLE TRY medication for insomnia. Some of the more common prescription sleeping pills are Ambien, Lunesta, Sonata, and Rozerem, with several other sleeping medications in the process of being developed. These medications have been found to have few negative effects, and recent studies indicate little tolerance over long periods, whereas in the past it was recommended that sleeping medications not be taken for more than two to three weeks. However, if you are pregnant or nursing, drugs are not a good solution to help you sleep at night (see "Sleeping Pills and Pregnancy," below).

There are also many over-the-counter sleeping pills available. Almost all of these, such as Tylenol PM and Simply Sleep, contain diphenhydramine (trade name, Benadryl). Many women find that diphenhydramine lasts in their system a long time and they feel hungover the next morning. There are also other medications sold in health food stores that are targeted at improving sleep, such as melatonin. You should not take any of these medications for sleep without first talking to your health care provider.

Sleeping Pills and Pregnancy

AT THIS TIME there are no medications that are approved by the Food and Drug Administration (FDA) that are considered completely safe for pregnant women. The FDA classifies the safety levels of medications for pregnant women based on the following class system:

- **CLASS A:** Controlled human studies have demonstrated no risks to the fetus.
- **CLASS B:** Presumed safe, based on animal studies; no well-controlled human studies are available.
- **CLASS C:** Safety is uncertain; data from human studies do not exist, and animal studies have shown some question of risk to the fetus. Pregnant women may take these medicines if they clearly need them.
- **CLASS D:** Evidence suggests the possibility of the medication causing birth defects or other problems, but a pregnant woman still might need to take it for her own medical needs.
- **CLASS X:** Proven risks to the fetus outweigh any possible benefits to the mother.

At this time, the medications approved for the treatment of insomnia are classified as follows:

- **BENADRYL (DIPHENHYDRAMINE):** Diphenhydramine is in the FDA pregnancy class B. This means that it is not expected to be harmful to an unborn baby.
- **AMBIEN (ZOLPIDEM):** Zolpidem is a Class B drug that is presumed safe when used during pregnancy.
- **SONATA (ZALEPLON):** Zaleplon is a Class C drug, meaning that it is not known whether it will harm an unborn baby.
- **LUNESTA (ESZOPICLONE):** Eszopiclone is a Class C drug, meaning that it is not known whether it will harm an unborn baby.
- **ROZEREM (RAMELTEON):** Ramelteon is in the FDA pregnancy class C. This means that it is not known whether Ramelteon will harm an unborn baby.

Do not take any of these medications if you are pregnant or nursing without first talking to your doctor.

Seven Rules for Beating Insomnia

STUDY AFTER STUDY has shown that if you diligently follow the seven rules outlined here, you can successfully fall sleep and stay asleep.

1. **CHOOSE A SET WAKE-UP TIME.** Wake up at exactly the same time every day, no matter how much sleep you got the night before.
2. **CHOOSE A BEDTIME.** Pick a bedtime that enables you to get the sleep you need. Spending too much time in bed will lead to

more interrupted sleep, so the best bedtime is one that allows you to get the sleep that you need but doesn't let you be in bed too long. You only want to spend the amount of time in bed that you actually need for sleep.

3. **GO TO BED WHEN YOU ARE SLEEPY, BUT NOT BEFORE YOUR CHOSEN BEDTIME.** Don't go to bed until you are sleepy. If you are still not sleepy at your chosen bedtime, wait until you are sleepy. This will help you to fall asleep quickly.

4. **GET OUT OF BED WHEN YOU CAN'T SLEEP.** If you are lying in bed and can't sleep, get out of bed and do something relaxing. It's best to also leave your bedroom. Read a book, listen to quiet music, or do something else relaxing, then go back to bed when you feel sleepy. Again, if you do not fall asleep quickly, get up. Keep repeating this cycle until you fall asleep. You need to get out of bed when you can't sleep at bedtime and in the middle of the night (that's the hard part!).

5. **DON'T WORRY OR PLAN IN BED.** When lying in bed at night, don't worry or plan for the next day. Set aside another time of the day to do these things. If you start thinking and worrying when you get in bed, get up. Don't head back to bed until you feel your thoughts won't interfere with falling asleep. Thinking in bed is a habit, and one that you can break.

6. **USE YOUR BED ONLY FOR SLEEP.** Don't do anything but sleep in your bed. That is, don't engage in other activities, such as eating, watching television, or paying bills in your bed (romance is allowed).

7. **AVOID NAPS.** If you have insomnia, taking a nap will make it difficult to fall asleep at bedtime. So, no naps.

Talk to Your Health Care Provider

BE SURE TO talk to your health care provider if you are having problems falling asleep, staying asleep, or waking too early. Don't expect insomnia to be a normal part of your life, whether or not you are pregnant. Instead, find solutions to help you get the sleep that you need.

Reminders

- Insomnia affects almost 80 percent of pregnant women and about 40 percent of new moms.
- The two main symptoms of insomnia are difficulty sleeping and daytime impairment.
- If worrying is keeping you up at night, write down your thoughts or share them with others. Try not to worry about sleep, and teach yourself to stop worrying.
- There are many things that you can do to help you fall asleep and stay asleep, from aromatherapy and warm baths to behavioral strategies such as relaxation and sleep restriction.
- Follow the seven rules for beating insomnia and you'll be getting the sleep that you need.

EIGHT

Restless Legs Syndrome and Periodic Limb Movement Disorder

> "It isn't that I'm not tired at bedtime, actually I'm utterly exhausted. But after a few minutes of lying in bed, my legs start to feel funny and I have to move them. I always end up getting out of bed and walking around the room, which obviously does not help me fall asleep."
> —*Kristen, 24 weeks pregnant*

> "It's the oddest feeling. I lie in bed at night and feel like I have to constantly move my legs."
> —*Kendra, 32 weeks pregnant*

Many pregnant (and nonpregnant) women have the same experience as Kristen and Kendra. They lie in bed (or ride in a car, or sit in a movie theater) and their legs start to feel uncomfortable. The only way to make them feel better is to move them. These feelings may be related to a sleep disorder called restless legs syndrome (RLS). Restless legs syndrome is characterized by an uncomfortable "creepy-crawly" feeling in the legs, usually below the knee, primarily when a person lies down to go to sleep. There is another sleep disorder that can be related to RLS that is called periodic limb movement disorder (PLMD). Periodic limb movement disorder is a condition in which a person's limbs, usually the legs, repetitively jerk or kick during sleep. Both of these sleep disturbances can be related to iron deficiency or low levels of folic acid, a common condition during pregnancy.

Restless Legs Syndrome (RLS)

Before she got pregnant, every once in a while Laura's legs bothered her at bedtime. What she found to be most helpful was to lie on her back in bed and "bicycle" her legs. However, now that she is pregnant, she's having problems every night. It's getting harder and harder for her to bicycle her legs with her growing belly, and her husband is beginning to think that she is nuts. She described it as "absolute torture." There was no other word that she could use to explain what it's like to lie in bed every night completely exhausted, with these incredibly uncomfortable feelings in her legs.

AS EXPLAINED ABOVE, restless legs syndrome is characterized by an uncomfortable feeling in your legs, usually below the knee, when you lie down to go to sleep. This feeling is often difficult to describe, but some people say that it is like "bugs crawling" or that it is "creepy-crawly"; others use words like "prickling," "tickling," and "itching." These sensations are alleviated by moving your legs while in bed, or you may find that you have to get out of bed to walk around or pace.

Do You Have RLS?

IF YOU ANSWER "yes" to the following question, there is a good chance that you have restless legs syndrome:

When you try to relax in the evening or sleep at night, do you ever have unpleasant, restless, or tickling feelings in your legs that can be relieved by walking or movement?

Stretching your legs can help. You may rub your legs or ask someone else to do it to make them feel better. Or you may just end up tossing and turning. Unfortunately, the symptoms return when you stop moving. (A list of things you can do to help appears on pages 166–67).

Ironically, the precise things that you need to do in order to fall asleep (relax and stay still) are the very same things that are most likely to cause your RLS symptoms. Conversely, activity and moving are the two things that may relieve your uncomfortable leg sensations, but these also make it nearly impossible to fall asleep. The result is difficulty falling asleep and insomnia.

RLS symptoms also can occur at other times of the day, mostly when sitting for long periods, such as at the movies or on long car rides. It doesn't have to happen only at night. Some women have RLS symptoms every night, and others on just some nights, often when they are particularly tired. Finally, RLS can also occur if you wake up during the night and can make it hard to fall back to sleep.

The symptoms of restless legs syndrome may include any or all of the following:

- **LEG DISCOMFORT.** The hallmark of RLS is uncomfortable feelings in your legs. These feelings usually occur at bedtime but can also occur at other times when you are sitting still, such as during long car or airplane rides or when watching a movie. You may find that these feelings are not actually "painful," but rather are just uncomfortable. Some people report that the feeling is inside or deep within their legs.

- **LEG MOVEMENTS.** To relieve the uncomfortable sensations in your legs, you may have an irresistible urge to move your legs, whether it is tossing and turning while lying in bed or walking about or pacing at bedtime. Vigorous movement, such as bicycling your legs, can also help.

- **SLEEP DISRUPTION.** It may take you a long time to fall asleep because of the leg discomfort and the need to move. You may also have problems staying asleep.

- **DAYTIME SLEEPINESS.** The difficulties with falling asleep and staying asleep can result in significant daytime sleepiness related to getting inadequate or poor quality sleep. So you may find it hard to wake up in the morning and/or you may feel sleepy during the day.

- **DIFFICULTY SITTING STILL.** You may have symptoms during the day, too, making it hard for you to sit still. This can occur during long car rides, plane flights, movies, or even during a long meeting at work. You may be constantly jiggling or moving your legs.

Words People Use to Describe Restless Legs Syndrome

Creepy	Gotta moves	Itchy bones	Itchy
Crawly	Heebie-Jeebies	Crazy legs	Bugs crawling
Pulling	Electric current	Worms crawling	
Jumpies	Prickling	Tickling	

Quiz

Screening Questionnaire for Restless Legs Syndrome (RLS)

DO YOU . . .	Yes	No
Complain of uncomfortable or funny feelings (creeping, crawling, tingling) in your legs?	_____	_____
Notice funny feelings in your legs (or they seem worse) when lying down or sitting?	_____	_____
Have partial relief with movement (wiggling feet, toes, or walking)?	_____	_____
Complain that the feelings are worse at night?	_____	_____
Have a lot of fidgeting or wiggling of your feet or toes when sitting or lying down?	_____	_____
Have repeated jerking movements in your toes or legs or your whole body while sleeping?	_____	_____
Appear restless while you are sleeping?	_____	_____

If you answered "yes" to two or more of these questions, be sure to speak to your doctor.

Periodic Limb Movement Disorder

Danielle couldn't understand why she always felt tired during the day. She was in bed by 10:00 every night and fell asleep quickly. However, she still had a hard time waking up in the morning at 6:30. Her husband often teased her that she was more active asleep than awake. There were times that it was so bad that he would go sleep in their spare bedroom just so he wouldn't get kicked all night.

Periodic limb movement disorder (PLMD) is a sleep disorder in which a person's limbs, usually her legs, repeatedly jerk or kick during sleep. This is also a movement disorder like restless legs syndrome, but one that occurs while you are sleeping rather than when you are trying to fall asleep. These movements tend to occur in spurts of at least several kicks or twitches in a row, at intervals of about 20 to 40 seconds. These clusters of movements can last from a few minutes to a few hours. Many times the person sleeps through the periodic limb movements, but they can also result in frequent brief awakenings or arousals throughout the night. You are unlikely to be aware of these arousals, as they can be as brief as 3 seconds—something you won't remember or even know about. At other times the leg movements can totally wake you up, and it will feel as if you are constantly waking up during the night but you don't know why. Waking up throughout the night, whether just briefly for 3 seconds or being up for a longer time, will make you feel sleepy the next day, since you are not getting quality sleep. Sometimes the only complaint of someone with PLMD is the daytime fatigue rather than the sleep symptoms themselves.

Unlike restless legs syndrome, you may or may not be aware of these leg movements. Rather, you may get complaints from you bed partner that you are an extremely restless sleeper or that you kick your legs during the night. To someone else, your movements may appear as brief muscle twitches, jerking movements, or simply an upward flexing of the feet rather than a full-blown kick. Others sometimes refuse to share a bed with someone with PLMD. If you sleep alone, you may find that your bed is often a total mess in the morning.

The symptoms of periodic limb movement disorder may include any of the following, although you may not report any symptoms because you are asleep when they occur:

- **LEG MOVEMENTS.** Although you will probably not be aware of these movements, repetitive leg movements in sleep characterize periodic limb movement disorder.
- **SLEEP DISRUPTION.** You may wake up at night, as a result of being awakened from the leg kicks.
- **RESTLESS SLEEP.** You may be a restless sleeper due to the leg movements and the frequent arousals. Your bedcovers may be highly disheveled during the night and in the morning.
- **DAYTIME SLEEPINESS.** The frequent arousals in sleep can result in significant daytime sleepiness. You may have difficulty waking up in the morning or may still feel tired, even when it seems as though you got enough sleep the night before.
- **WORK PROBLEMS.** You may have problems concentrating and getting your work done, which is the result of the disrupted sleep.

RLS, PLMA, or Both?

RESTLESS LEGS SYNDROME and periodic limb movement disorder often occur together. Studies in adults indicate that 70 to 90 percent of adults with restless legs syndrome have periodic limb movement disorder. In contrast, only 20 to 30 percent of people with periodic limb movement disorder also have restless legs syndrome. Comparable studies have not been conducted with pregnant women, but it is expected that the relationship between these two sleep disorders is similar.

How Common Are RLS and PLMD During Pregnancy?

RLS IS RELATIVELY common in the general population, and even more common during pregnancy. Studies show that about one in four women (23 percent) have RLS during pregnancy, although some studies have reported it being as low as 1 in 10 women (11 percent) and others find it in 1 in 3 pregnant women (33 percent). This is in comparison to about 14 percent (about 1 in 7 women) in those who are beyond their childbearing years. In most cases, women have experienced some RLS prior to being pregnant, but in others it develops for the first time during pregnancy. Surprisingly, when the RLS is familial—that is it seems to be hereditary and runs in a specific woman's family—it is more likely to show up for the first time during pregnancy.

Although we don't know exactly how many people have PLMD, we do know that the prevalence increases with age. For example, 44 percent of individuals over the age of 60 experience PLMD compared to 5 percent of those between 30 and 50. Surprisingly, we do not know the percentage of women who are pregnant who have PLMD, as those studies have rarely been done. It's easier to study the prevalence of RLS than PLMD, because to find out whether a woman has PLMD, she would need to have an overnight sleep study. RLS is based instead on just the reporting of symptoms. One study, however, reported that PLMD is almost universal in pregnant women.

Although these sleep problems are common, they are not

commonly diagnosed. In the general population, despite the fact that one in every ten adults has RLS, many people have symptoms for years before they are diagnosed. Some are never diagnosed at all. There's a bit of a conspiracy of silence to account for this. Patients don't think their symptoms are related to a medical condition, or they may embarrassed by them, and so they don't bring them to the attention of their doctor. Doctors often know very little about these disorders and rarely ask about potential symptoms.

What Causes These Conditions?

No one knows what exactly causes RLS, although in many women, especially pregnant women, it is often related to anemia (low iron) or low levels of folate (folic acid). It is often more likely related to low levels of serum folate, so be sure to be tested for this in addition to iron. Hormonal changes may also contribute to the development of these sleep disorders, but we do not actually know what role they play. PLMD is the same, as it, too, can be related to low levels of iron or folic acid.

RLS can run in families, which means in these cases it's probably genetic. Most adults with restless legs syndrome have a family member with the same disorder, and the risk of developing RLS is 6 to 7 times higher in close relatives of those with RLS. As said above, surprisingly, when the RLS is genetic, it often shows up for the first time when a woman is pregnant.

Finally, there are some things that can exacerbate both problems. Caffeine, alcohol, and some medications can all make RLS and PLMD worse. Obstructive sleep apnea (see chapter 9) can also trigger periodic limb movements during sleep.

Common symptoms of restless legs syndrome and periodic limb movement disorder

AT BEDTIME

Difficulty falling asleep

Leg movements

Walking or pacing

Leg pain

Leg discomfort

DURING THE NIGHT

Leg movements

Restless sleep

Nighttime awakenings

DURING THE DAY

Daytime sleepiness

Difficulty waking up in the morning

Morning grogginess

Falling asleep at work or at inappropriate times

Need to nap

Mood changes: irritability, impatience, mood swings, depression/anxiety

Leg movements when sitting still or lying down

Inability to sit still for long periods

Leg discomfort

Making the Diagnosis

RESTLESS LEGS SYNDROME. There is no definitive test for restless legs syndrome, so a diagnosis is made based on the description of symptoms. A screening questionnaire can be found on page 157. To evaluate for RLS, your doctor will take a medical history and do a physical examination to exclude other problems. Finally, an overnight sleep study may be recommended to evaluate for other sleep disorders, especially periodic limb movement disorder, since these two disorders often go hand in hand. Blood work will be ordered to check for iron deficiency anemia with a specific test called a ferritin level test.

PERIODIC LIMB MOVEMENT DISORDER. Periodic limb movement disorder is diagnosed with an overnight sleep study. You will need to stay overnight in a sleep laboratory, and the number of leg movements will be measured throughout the night while you sleep. You may be told the severity of your PLMD, which is based on your periodic limb movement index. This term refers to the average number of times that you have these movements per hour. So if you slept for 8 hours and you moved your legs a total of 80 times, your periodic limb movement index would be 10 (80 times divided by 8 hours). In addition, they will calculate your periodic limb movement arousal index, which is a similar measure of your periodic limb movements per hour that were associated with an arousal (meaning your brain woke up). Periodic limb movements that do not lead to an arousal are of much less concern. Mild PLMD is defined as 5 to 25 periodic limb movements per hour of sleep, moderate PLMD equals 25 to 50 times per hour, and severe is more than 50 times per hour for periodic limb movements or 25 times per hour for periodic limb movements that are associated with an arousal. In addition to the overnight sleep study, your doctor will take a complete medical history and will conduct a physical exam. As with RLS, your doctor will want to check your iron and ferritin levels.

What Else Could It Be?

THERE ARE MANY other things that could be causing you pain or discomfort in your legs, or leading to problems sleeping.

- **LEG CRAMPS.** Leg cramps are very common during pregnancy. During a leg cramp, your calf muscle will severely tighten and you'll experience pain. These leg cramps usually come on suddenly.

Leg Cramps

LEG CRAMPS ARE quite different from RLS and PLMD. Leg cramps are actual muscle cramps in your leg or foot. They last a specific amount of time and then go away. Leg cramps can be excruciatingly painful. They are also very common during pregnancy. Below are prevalence rates that have been found across several studies.

Before pregnancy	8–10 percent of women
1st trimester	12–21 percent of women
2nd trimester	49–57 percent of women
3rd trimester	73–75 percent of women

Chapter 6 provides information on what you can do to prevent and minimize leg cramps.

- **PINS AND NEEDLES.** Especially during pregnancy, your legs (and other parts of your body) may "fall asleep," giving you the feeling of having pins and needles in your arms or legs. Changing position will help this feeling go away.
- **ANOTHER SLEEP DISORDER.** Taking a long time to fall asleep at night and waking up at night may result from insomnia (see chapter 7 for more information on insomnia).
- **DAYTIME SLEEPINESS.** Being sleepy can be caused by many other things, including another sleep disorder, like obstructive sleep apnea, narcolepsy, and simply not getting enough sleep. During pregnancy, you are also more likely to feel sleepy during the day, related to hormonal changes.
- **UNCOMFORTABLE LEG SENSATIONS.** Your leg discomfort can be related to many other things, including sore muscles, orthopedic problems, or chronic pain from something like arthritis.
- **RESTLESS SLEEP.** It is common during pregnancy to be restless throughout the night. Sleep apnea may be the cause of nighttime restlessness (see chapter 9). Sheer discomfort, especially in the third trimester, may wake you up throughout the night.

What You Can Do

Janine found that it took a combination of things to help relieve her RLS. She developed RLS during her previous pregnancy, so she was expecting to have problems again. She started having her iron levels tested regularly by her obstetrician. She also cut out all caffeine,

including her usual morning cup of coffee, which she dearly missed.
Finally, she tried to go for a brisk evening walk with her 2-year-old
daughter in a jogging stroller as often as she could. Not only did it
seem to help the uncomfortable feelings that she got in her legs at
bedtime, it was also a good way to exercise and help her daughter
settle down for bedtime.

THERE ARE A number of things that can be helpful to relieve
the symptoms of restless legs syndrome and/or periodic limb
movement disorder.

- **IRON AND/OR FOLIC ACID.** For many women, especially
  women who are pregnant, the RLS or PLMD is related to an iron deficiency (anemia) or low levels of folic
  acid. These can be detected with a blood test. In these
  cases, the treatment is simple: take iron or folic acid
  supplements. Serum ferritin levels are recommended to
  be above 40–50 mcg/L, if possible, during pregnancy.
- **TAKE A BATH.** Some women find that taking a bath
  before bedtime helps. Some women find that a hot
  bath helps, whereas other women prefer a cold bath.
  Be careful, though, about taking very hot baths while
  pregnant. As with everything, check first with your
  health care provider.
- **GET MORE SLEEP.** Getting adequate sleep will also help.
  Sleep deprivation will make these problems worse.
- **WAIT TO GET IN BED.** If you have RLS, the longer you
  lie in bed, the worse your legs will feel. So don't get
  into bed until you are ready to turn out the lights and
  go to sleep. Try to avoid reading in bed or watching
  television while lying in bed. It's best to engage in
  those activities elsewhere.

- **PHYSICAL ACTIVITY.** If moving your legs helps your RLS, then move them. Some women find that engaging in vigorous activity just prior to going to bed can help a lot. You may not have to be that active, though. Instead, try stretching exercises right before bed.

- **EXERCISE.** Some women find that their symptoms fluctuate with the amount of exercise they get. A mild or moderate amount of exercise helps. On the other hand, a burst of vigorous exercise or a period of no activity can make symptoms worse.

- **DISTRACT YOURSELF.** The more you lie and think about your legs, the worse it will get. So try distracting yourself, especially if you are having problems during the day. Read an engrossing book, do needlework, write the novel that you always meant to start, or just daydream about your favorite vacation spot.

- **MASSAGE YOUR LEGS.** Many women find that massaging their legs can help a lot. Even better, get your bed partner to massage your legs. You may end up getting two bonuses in one—a massage and being distracted!

- **REDUCE THE DISCOMFORT.** Cold compresses or a heating pad may give you temporary relief of the uncomfortable sensations of restless legs syndrome. Walking and stretching can also help.

- **MEDICATIONS.** For many people, medications are prescribed, such as pramipexole (Mirapex), ropinirole (Requip), pergolide (Permax), and carbidopa/levodopa (Sinemet). Note that there are no drugs that are used to treat RLS or PLMD that are considered to be completely safe to be taken during pregnancy. Some drugs are considered to be of lower risk than others. Always discuss these issues with your health care provider before taking any medications while you are pregnant, including over-the-counter medications that you would purchase at a drug store or a health food store. The same is the case if you are nursing; be sure to speak to your doctor before taking any medications while nursing.

What to Avoid

JUST AS THERE are things that you can do to treat RLS and PLMD, there are also things that you should avoid. All of these things can make these two sleep disorders worse.

- **HEAVY COVERS.** Sleeping under heavy covers or a comforter can make your RLS and PLMD worse. Instead use lighter-weight blankets. Fortunately, there are many wonderful bedding choices these days, especially with all the different fleece blankets available.
- **CAFFEINE.** Caffeine makes RLS and PLMD much worse, so avoid any coffee, tea, iced tea, and caffeinated sodas, especially after lunchtime. Read labels carefully, as many drinks contain caffeine that you may not expect, such as some orange sodas and some energy drinks.
- **ALCOHOL.** Again, if you are pregnant or nursing, you should be avoiding alcohol in the first place. Alcohol can also make symptoms worse, so stay away from that glass of wine or cocktail in the evening. Alcohol may help you fall asleep initially, but after an hour or so it can make your symptoms much worse than normal.

- **NICOTINE.** You shouldn't be smoking anyway, but nicotine has also been found to make RLS and PLMD worse. Nicotine is a stimulant and can exacerbate RLS and PLMD.

- **OTHER MEDICATIONS.** There are also some medications that you may be taking for other issues that can make RLS and PLMD worse, such as antihistamines, cold/sinus preparations, and anti-nausea medications. In addition, some antidepressants can make PLMD worse. If you are taking any other medication, talk to your doctor so that the proper combination of treatments can be utilized.

After the Baby Is Born

FOR MOST WOMEN, both RLS and PLMD will disappear after the baby is born. Approximately 15 to 20 percent of women will continue to have problems postpartum, meaning that 80 to 85 percent of women will no longer have symptoms of RLS. So expect the problems to go away if you just developed RLS and/or PLMD when you were pregnant, but definitely talk to your doctor if your symptoms persist. You will have more choices of treatment when you are no longer pregnant and not nursing.

Talk to Your Health Care Provider

BE SURE TO speak to your health care provider if your legs feel uncomfortable at bedtime and you feel the need to move them or you frequently kick your legs while you sleep.

Reminders

- Restless legs syndrome (RLS) is an uncomfortable sensation in your legs, primarily occurring at bedtime, that improves if you move your legs.
- Periodic limb movement disorder (PLMD) is leg kicking or jerking while you are asleep. These leg movements can interrupt your sleep.
- During pregnancy, RLS develops in about 1 out of every 4 women. It often occurs with PLMD.
- The most common causes of RLS and PLMD during pregnancy are low iron or low levels of folic acid. Iron and folic acid supplements can help tremendously.
- Other things that can help include warm baths, avoiding caffeine, and exercising regularly.
- RLS and PLMD usually disappear once the baby is born.

NINE

Snoring and Sleep Apnea

"It is so embarrassing. I snore like a truck driver."
—Melanie, 21 weeks pregnant

"I have lost all sense of feeling feminine. I waddle during the day, I have absolutely no figure, and now I snore like an old man at night—with my mouth hanging open and snoring so loudly that my 4-year-old daughter even complains from the next room."
—Christina, 32 weeks pregnant

Do you snore? Lots of women snore, although most won't admit it in public. Snoring itself isn't really bad for you (although it often bothers everyone else in the household), but it can be a sign of a more serious sleep problem called sleep apnea. Although these two sleep problems often occur together, in that most women with sleep apnea snore, it is important to note that not all women who snore have sleep apnea. In addition to sleep apnea not being good for your body, it's going to make you feel sleep deprived the next day, even if you thought you slept for eight or more hours the night before.

Snoring and sleep apnea often develop during pregnancy or get worse throughout pregnancy. Luckily, they usually go away once the baby is born—that is, if you didn't snore or have sleep apnea before.

Snoring

Jessica, pregnant with her third child, moved into the spare bedroom because her snoring was so loud that it kept her husband awake. She finds it very embarrassing, especially when he jokes that every time she is pregnant, he gets his very own bachelor pad.

SNORING IS VERY prevalent during pregnancy. Depending on the study, somewhere between 25 and 30 percent of women snore by the end of pregnancy. That is, almost 1 out of 3 or 4 women snore. In contrast, only about 4 percent of women report snoring before becoming pregnant. So becoming a snorer while pregnant is not uncommon. In addition, snoring usually gets worse as pregnancy progresses, especially in the third trimester.

Snoring is caused by the muscles of the airway relaxing during sleep. When the muscles become relaxed, they have a tendency to flap (like a sail not pulled taut in the wind). Snoring is the sound of the muscles flapping. Most snoring occurs when the person is inhaling.

Some pregnant women snore every night and throughout the night, whereas others snore just once in a while. Snoring is more likely to occur when you lie on your back, but it can occur in any sleep position. Many women are not even aware that they snore unless others tell them (including the neighbors). Others snore so loudly that they even wake themselves.

How loud is loud? Just ask anybody who lives with a snorer. Snoring averages about 60 decibels and can be as noisy as 80 decibels. To give you some perspective, normal speech is about

40 decibels. A whisper is about 30 decibels. A baby crying is about 60 decibels. A vacuum cleaner is about 70 decibels. Eighty decibels is similar to a large dog barking. Some people's snoring is so loud that the noise they generate exceeds government standards for noise in the workplace!

Once the Baby Is Born

MOST WOMEN—60 PERCENT—WHO snore during pregnancy find that they no longer snore soon after their baby is born. However, the other 40 percent of new moms are still snoring. Weight is likely a contributor to whether the snoring goes away. If you are still carrying around your baby weight, you are more likely to be snoring. And obviously, if you snored before you were pregnant, you will likely still snore after the baby is born.

What Causes Snoring?

The most common cause of snoring during pregnancy is weight gain. As you gain weight during pregnancy, you may become bulkier around your neck. A larger neck can decrease the size of the airway, which can contribute to snoring. Allergies and colds also can lead to snoring, since nasal congestion forces you to breathe through your mouth.

Swollen nasal passages are common during pregnancy and can also cause snoring. One reason for this is the higher level of estrogen in your body, which increases swelling in the lining of your nose. Likewise, during pregnancy the amount of blood your body produces increases and your blood vessels expand, both of which can lead to swollen nasal membranes.

Does Snoring Matter?

Snoring should not be ignored. Some people believe that snoring is a sign of being a "good sleeper." This is not true. Snoring really isn't "normal," but it isn't harmful, except maybe to your marriage. Many couples sleep in separate bedrooms because one person's snoring chases the other out of the bedroom.

For others, however, snoring can actually be a symptom of a more serious sleep disorder–sleep apnea (which is discussed below). One way to tell if you have sleep apnea is to determine whether you are sleepier during the day than you should be, given the amount of sleep that you get. Women with sleep apnea are often very sleepy during the day, even after getting 7 or 8 hours of sleep.

Even if the snoring is not affecting your health, you still may wish to seek treatment, especially if your bed partner isn't getting any sleep. There are hundreds of devices available that claim to stop snoring. Most try to keep the mouth closed or open the nasal airway. Such devices include bandages that go over the nose (such as Breathe Right) or prongs that widen the nose. Unfortunately, many of these devices do not always work. Other devices try to keep you off your back, since many people snore only when on their back. An easier and cheaper alternative is simply to sew a pocket onto the back of a pajama top or T-shirt and place a tennis ball in it. Other more elaborate and expensive methods include alarms that go off when you roll over onto your back. These devices are only effective if you snore when on your back.

Sleep Apnea

Anne is 34 years old and snored once in a while before she was pregnant, but only if she had a cold. Now, though, her snoring has gotten much worse. Many nights her husband ends up sleeping in the living room because her snoring is so loud. Anne never feels rested in the morning or as if she has gotten a good night's sleep. She finds herself putting her head down on her desk at work and taking quick naps several times throughout the day. The worst was when her boss walked into her office and found her asleep.

ANNE IS A classic example of someone who has sleep apnea. Sleep apnea can develop during pregnancy because of increased nasal congestion, weight gain, and increased relaxation of the muscles due to hormonal changes. Sleep apnea is a breathing disorder in which a person has repetitive episodes of upper airway obstruction during sleep. These fancy words mean that numerous times throughout the night you stop breathing because your airway closes. These events cause you to wake up frequently throughout the night. You may not be aware of these awakenings, because it is often for just a few seconds. To be diagnosed with sleep apnea, you must stop breathing at least 5 times per hour. However, most women with sleep apnea stop breathing many more times than that. For example, there are some women who stop breathing more than 50 or even 100 times per hour. Basically, these women can't sleep and breathe at the same time. Every time they fall asleep, they stop breathing. Luckily, our brains are wired to sound the alarm every time we stop breathing, so you will always wake up after each apneic event. But you'll end up feeling exhausted the next day.

How Common Is Sleep Apnea During Pregnancy?

Catherine is 6 months pregnant and is feeling more and more tired every day. Every morning she wakes up feeling as tired as when she went to bed. Her husband says that her snoring is louder than ever, and at least a few times a night he pokes her to make sure that she is still breathing.

Studies indicate that more than 10 percent of pregnant women develop sleep apnea during pregnancy. For example, one study found that choking awakenings, a common symptom of sleep apnea, increase from 6 percent of women in their first trimester to 34 percent in their third trimester.

As with snoring, the primary causes of sleep apnea during pregnancy are weight gain and increased nasal congestion. Studies have also shown that there is a narrowing of the upper airways (the air passages to your nose and mouth), especially during the third trimester of pregnancy. Again, this is related to increased blood and expansion of blood vessels during pregnancy, weight gain, and increased estrogen levels.

Symptoms of Sleep Apnea

Some pregnant women have all of the symptoms listed below, whereas others have only a few. Most women with sleep apnea don't even know that they have a problem. Usually it is a bed partner who suspects a problem or is bothered enough by it to force the person to seek help.

- **SNORING.** As said above, most people with sleep apnea snore. Not all snorers, though, have sleep apnea. For pregnant women, sleep apnea occurs in a little over 10 percent of women who habitually snore, compared to just 2 percent of pregnant women who do not frequently snore.

- **BREATHING PAUSES.** Sleep apnea is characterized by breathing pauses. A person will stop breathing anywhere from 10 seconds to, at the most, 45 seconds. To start breathing again, the person must first wake up, although they will rarely know that they woke up.

- **DAYTIME SLEEPINESS.** The one symptom that is almost universal to sleep apnea, and the only one many women are often aware of, is daytime sleepiness. The daytime sleepiness is caused by the numerous arousals throughout the night. It is almost like being poked every five minutes throughout the entire night. Some women with sleep apnea are so sleepy that they fall asleep during sex, while driving, and even in the midst of conversations.

- **COUGHING AND CHOKING DURING SLEEP.** Some women with sleep apnea find that they wake up during the night coughing and choking.

- **DRY MOUTH.** Many women with sleep apnea wake up with a dry mouth. This is because they are breathing and snoring with their mouth open.

- **MORNING HEADACHES.** Another common symptom of sleep apnea is a headache in the morning. Usually by midmorning the headache has gone away.

- **RESTLESS SLEEP.** Because of the frequent arousals throughout the night, a woman with sleep apnea appears to be a restless sleeper. With each arousal the woman may move her legs or roll over (if she still can roll over!). In addition, you may find that your bedcovers are all over the place when you wake up in the morning.

Other common symptoms include:

- **INSOMNIA.** Surprisingly, some people with sleep apnea complain of insomnia. Although they are extremely sleepy and tired, they are unable to fall asleep at night. This is because they stop breathing as they are falling asleep. When the breathing pause occurs, they have an arousal and wake up. The insomnia is, thus, caused by the breathing problems.
- **DAYTIME FATIGUE AND IRRITABILITY.** Another common complaint of women with sleep apnea is that they don't feel that they function well during the day. They may become forgetful. They may feel irritable, anxious, or depressed.

Are You at Risk for Developing Snoring and Sleep Apnea?

IT IS HARD to predict which women will have problems with snoring and/or sleep apnea during pregnancy. Almost any woman can experience either problem at any time during pregnancy. However, there are a few things that will increase your risk. These risk factors include:

- **EXCESSIVE WEIGHT GAIN.** Weight is a major contributor to snoring and sleep apnea in all women, not just those who are pregnant. All pregnant women will gain weight, but if you gain too much weight, you will be more likely to snore and have nighttime breathing problems.

- **OBESITY.** Irrespective of how much weight, you gain, if you are overweight or obese, it will increase your risk of snoring and sleep apnea.
- **NECK SIZE.** Women who snore tend to have a neck size that is larger than women who do not snore. Men often know their neck size for purchasing dress shirts, but most women do not know theirs nor think that much about their neck size. Basically, if you have a large neck, then you are at increased risk.
- **ASTHMA OR ALLERGIES.** Those women with asthma and/or allergies are also at increased risk, as any type of breathing problems are going to increase the likelihood of snoring and sleep apnea.

Obese Women

IF YOU ARE obese, you need to be extra careful, as you are more likely to snore and have sleep apnea. One study compared two groups of pregnant women—one group who was obese prior to getting pregnant and one group who was not. At the end of the first trimester, 32 percent of the obese women snored compared to just 1 percent of the non-obese women. By the end of pregnancy, this difference was even more dramatic, with 39 percent of the obese women snoring and still only 1 percent of the non-obese women. Few of these women had sleep apnea. So if you are overweight or obese, be sure to discuss your breathing at night with your doctor. Tell your family to let you know if you start snoring or have any problems breathing when you are asleep.

Impact of Snoring and Sleep
Apnea During Pregnancy

MOST WOMEN WHO snore or have sleep apnea during pregnancy are fine and their babies are born perfectly healthy. However, snoring and sleep apnea have been linked to some potential complications.

SWELLING. Swelling (the fancy word is *edema*) is more common in pregnant women who snore. One study found that swelling of the face, hands, legs, or feet occurred in 52 percent of pregnant women who were habitual snorers, compared to 30 percent of pregnant women who did not snore.

HIGH BLOOD PRESSURE AND PREECLAMPSIA. Preeclampsia is a condition characterized by increased blood pressure, protein in the urine, and swelling that affects about 7 percent of all pregnant women, typically occurring after 20 weeks. Pregnant women with preeclampsia may also have daytime sleepiness, headaches, vision problems, and vomiting.

The cause of preeclampsia is unknown. However, it can be associated with snoring. In one study of 500 pregnant women, 14 percent of the women who snored developed high blood pressure, and 10 percent were diagnosed with preeclampsia, compared to just 6 percent and 4 percent, respectively, of the women who did not snore. In addition, snoring may predict the later development of preeclampsia. Remember, looking at the numbers above, almost all women who snore do *not* develop high blood pressure (86 percent do not develop high blood pressure) or preeclampsia (90 percent do not develop preeclampsia). But if you do snore, it is smart to let your health care practitioner know so that you and your baby can be more closely monitored.

GROWTH OF THE BABY. Snoring and sleep apnea seem to put a few babies at risk for growth problems. For example, in one study 7 percent of infants born to mothers who snored were considered small for their age, compared to almost 3 percent of infants whose mothers did not snore. Although twice as many babies of mothers who snored were small for their age, these data also indicate that 93 percent of infants of mothers who snored were fine.

Making the Diagnosis

THE ONLY WAY to know for sure whether you have sleep apnea is to have an overnight sleep study, referred to as a *polysomnogram.* This is a test that usually takes place overnight in a sleep clinic. An overnight sleep study incorporates measurements of your sleep and your breathing, as well as other factors such as your heart rate. Electrodes will be glued on or taped on (nothing is stuck in you!). Surprisingly, most people sleep fine during a sleep study. It usually takes a week or two to get your results. At that point, your doctor will determine if you have sleep apnea and what's the best treatment for it.

What You Can Do

FIRST, REMEMBER THAT sleep apnea is a serious problem that should not be ignored. Be sure to talk to your health care provider if you snore or have any problems breathing during the night (or someone tells you that you do). Unfortunately, sleep apnea often goes untreated in many women, either because they don't recognize they have sleep apnea or because they discount their symptoms, believing that "everyone snores."

There are a number of things that you can try yourself to help reduce snoring and/or sleep apnea. In addition, there are a number of things that you should avoid so that your snoring and/or sleep apnea doesn't get worse.

SLEEP ON YOUR SIDE. Often snoring and sleep apnea are much worse when sleeping on your back. So as much as possible, try to sleep on your side. That's the most comfortable position anyway during pregnancy, and the best sleep position for your baby.

ELEVATE YOUR HEAD. You may also find it helpful to elevate your head, even when sleeping on your side. Use an extra pillow or a sleeping wedge. You can even elevate the end of your bed, using a wedge that goes under your mattress, or simply putting the feet of one end of your bed up on bricks.

AVOID ALCOHOL. As always, you shouldn't be drinking alcohol during pregnancy, and alcohol will make snoring and sleep apnea worse. Alcohol acts as a sedative, relaxing your muscles even more while you sleep.

AVOID SLEEPING PILLS. Anything that makes your muscles relax is going to make snoring and sleep apnea worse. Sleeping pills often act as relaxants, making the muscles in your neck floppier, and making you more likely to snore or have breathing problems. If you are pregnant, you should already be avoiding sleeping pills. But even if you're not pregnant, it's still important to avoid them if you are having any breathing issues when you are sleeping.

DON'T GAIN TOO MUCH WEIGHT. Try not to gain more than the recommended amount of weight during pregnancy (about 25 to 35 pounds if your weight was normal before pregnancy). Obesity and weight gain are linked to snoring and sleep apnea in all adults. It's even more of an issue when you are pregnant.

Obviously, you need to gain weight during pregnancy for the health of your baby. Just try to stay within the recommended guidelines. Be sure to talk to your doctor about how to maintain a balanced diet during pregnancy.

ALLERGIES AND NASAL CONGESTION. Talk to your doctor about what you can do to help relieve any allergies and nasal congestion. Saline nasal sprays can be helpful for nasal congestion. In addition, using hypoallergenic pillows, comforters, and vinyl mattress and pillow covers can help. Vacuuming your bedroom thoroughly and reducing dust as much as possible can be helpful. Using an air purifier in your bedroom, regularly washing your bedding (including pillows), and replacing filters in furnaces and air conditions can also improve allergies. Finally, sleeping with your cat or dog, although wonderful for cuddling, may make your nasal congestion worse. It may be time to find them a better place to sleep in your home.

> *Marissa, pregnant with her third child, found that her snoring was getting louder and louder with each passing month. She decided she had to do something about it. First, she thoroughly cleaned her bedroom and washed all the bedding on her bed, including the pillows. She bought an air purifier for her room and, against her husband's wishes, had the dog sleep elsewhere in the house. She was amazed at what a difference just these few changes really made.*

Medical Treatments

> *Adelaide was 29 weeks pregnant. Her sister, with whom she shared a room while visiting relatives, told her that her breathing during the night was "downright scary." Several times she thought she was going to have shake Adelaide during the night to make sure she was breath-*

ing. Adelaide's doctor ordered an overnight sleep study and called her several days later with the results: she had severe sleep apnea. After taking a week or two to get used to using a CPAP (continuous positive airway pressure) machine, she couldn't believe how much better she felt in the morning. She previously had thought she was so tired just from being pregnant.

THERE ARE A number of medically based treatment options available for snoring and sleep apnea. The best treatment for you will depend on the severity of your snoring or sleep apnea, what is contributing to your symptoms, and what will work best for you.

- **CONTINUOUS POSITIVE AIRWAY PRESSURE (CPAP).** For most people with sleep apnea, CPAP is the treatment of choice. CPAP involves a machine that has a mask attached to it. There are two primary types of masks, one that is worn over the nose and one with pillows that are placed in the nose. The purpose of CPAP is to keep the airway open so that normal breathing can occur. The CPAP machine generates air pressure, and this air pressure is forced down the nose, causing the airway to stay open. CPAP machines can be set at different pressures. An overnight test will need to be conducted at a sleep center to find a pressure that is optimal for you—one that gets rid of snoring, decreases apnea, and does not interfere with your sleep. Many insurance companies will pay for CPAP as part of your medical coverage. Many women are surprised at how much better they feel after using CPAP.
- **SURGERY.** There are a number of surgical options available to treat sleep apnea. Obviously, though, this is

not an appropriate option for pregnant women. If you continue, though, to have problems with snoring and sleep apnea after the baby is born, you may want to consider surgery as a potential treatment. An ENT doctor will provide expertise in this area.

- **DENTAL APPLIANCE.** Some people with mild to moderate sleep apnea benefit from a dental appliance. Similar to ones used for people who grind their teeth in their sleep, this appliance is worn at night and it moves the lower jaw slightly forward. Moving the jaw forward helps keep the airway open and will decrease both snoring and sleep apnea. The use of a dental appliance on a nightly basis does not cause any jaw problems, which is a common concern. A dentist or orthodontist usually fits this device, which can be expensive. Unfortunately, many medical insurance policies will not cover the cost.

Talk to Your Health Care Provider

BE SURE TO talk to your health care provider if you snore or have any problems breathing during the night (or someone tells you that you do).

Reminders

- Snoring and sleep apnea often develop during pregnancy. Between 25 and 30 percent of women snore by the end of pregnancy, and about 10 percent develop sleep apnea.
- Snoring can be a sign of sleep apnea, a breathing problem that occurs when you are asleep.
- Other symptoms of sleep apnea include breathing pauses, daytime sleepiness, and restless sleep. Snoring and sleep apnea have been found to be associated with high blood pressure and preeclampsia, so be sure to talk to your health care provider.
- Sleeping on your side, elevating your head, not gaining too much weight, and managing allergies and nasal congestion can help. There are also several medical treatments available for pregnant women, including nasal CPAP and dental appliances.
- Fortunately, snoring and sleep apnea usually go away once the baby is born.

PART IV

After the

Baby Is Born

TEN

The First Six Weeks

"Greg and I knew that it would be hard having a newborn in the house, but after five weeks of no sleep, we are both starting to lose it. We even started fighting all the time, which we never did before. Although I hate to admit it, I sometimes wondered whether having a baby was the right decision."
—*Tonya, mom of a 5-week-old*

"I would do anything for just one good night's sleep. I feel like a total zombie all the time and I must look a wreck."
—*Sherie, mom of a 3-month-old*

Your baby has arrived! Although there is nothing more exciting, the first days and weeks at home with a newborn are sure to be overwhelming, whether or not you're a first-time mom. Babies always seem to cry and fuss at the most inconvenient times—just when you are scrambling to make dinner or right after you have finally fallen asleep at night. And while we experts claim that newborns can sleep for up to eighteen hours a day, somehow no one in the house seems to get any sleep.

One Mom's Advice

"If there was one piece of advice I would give new moms, it's to get sleep when you can!"

—*Michelle, mother of 6-month-old Aidan*

Surviving (and Enjoying) the First Six Weeks

EVERYONE PORTRAYS HAVING a new baby as a blissful experience—and it is! However, the first six weeks with a new baby can also be stressful. This is especially true with your first baby, because it's a major lifestyle change and you have a bunch to learn about the day-to-day basics of taking care of a baby. It is, however, also true with later-born children, because you now have to deal with balancing the needs of your newborn against the demands of your other children. It is all relative. Many parents with a firstborn are overwhelmed by the demands of a newborn. On the other hand, parents who have more than one child often say they didn't realize how easy they had it when they only had one.

Labor and Delivery

You should expect to feel exhausted when your brand-new bundle of joy arrives. Lack of sleep ramps up during the third trimester and then gets compounded during labor and delivery. Being in labor for hours on end, especially if you are in labor in the wee hours of the morning, will start you off sleep deprived.

In addition, women usually do not get a good night's sleep the first night after they deliver. Physically, you will likely be exhausted and sore, and your milk is coming in whether you are nursing or not. If you delivered in a hospital, expect to have your sleep disrupted continually. Nurses, doctors, and educators will likely be in and out of your room throughout the day and night.

And, most important, you have a brand-new baby to take

care of! Many new moms have their newborns room in with them if they deliver in a hospital. Some find it best to have their baby nearby, to facilitate breast-feeding and so that they are not worrying about whether their baby is okay. If you decide to have your baby room with you, try to have someone stay with you who can help care for the baby while you get some sleep.

You may, however, consider sending your baby to the nursery for a few hours so you can catch up on sleep. Ask the nurses to wake you when the baby needs to be fed or simply needs her mommy. Once you get home, you'll be on baby duty 24-hours a day, so it can be nice to have professional help the first night.

In addition, realize that it's okay to be tired and emotional. You've just gone through one of the most strenuous events of your life, whether you were in labor for just 6 hours or over 30. If you had a cesarean section, you went through major surgery. Either way, some of your hormones are plummeting from no longer being pregnant, and others are surging if you are nursing. And on top of it all, you likely haven't had more than a few hours of continuous sleep.

Coping with Change

Once you get home from the hospital, expect life to be topsy-turvy for at least the first few weeks. We all hope to have an easy baby who sleeps a lot and is placid when awake. Don't be surprised, though, if your newborn one day wakes up and all of a sudden requires a great deal of attention. Many newborns want to be held all the time. Investing in a baby sling or front pack can be a tremendous help. It will allow you to carry your baby while keeping your hands free.

Feeling unproductive is another factor that can make the first six weeks difficult. Getting anything done can seem impossible at times. You will be amazed at how quickly the day comes and goes and you haven't even managed to get a load of laundry done. Taking a trip to the grocery store or even the doctor is a major event—getting both you and the baby dressed, gathering all the paraphernalia you will need for a short outing (think diapers, bottles, pacifiers, extra clothes for everyone), and wrestling your baby into a car seat. Feeling this out of control of your life is especially hard on women who are used to having complete control over their lives and are used to multitasking all day long.

Furthermore, you may be having a difficult time sorting out who you are exactly, which is especially true for first-time moms. Often your very identity is tied to your job, whether you are a lawyer, doctor, office worker, or chef. Suddenly that has disappeared, and you are now simply a diaper-changing, baby-burping, fussy-baby-calming entity.

If you are nursing, your body no longer seems like your own either. It is no surprise that many new moms no longer feel like themselves. In addition, all it takes is seeing another new mom in the grocery store who is elegantly dressed, holding a baby in an adorable outfit with no spit-up stains, to make you feel totally inadequate. Never judge a book by its cover, though. That mom may very well have been home crying just a few hours ago.

Fatigue

Ten days after she delivered her daughter, Deanna felt as if she had zero energy. She could barely drag herself out of bed in the morning and couldn't get up the energy even to take a shower. A high-powered corporate attorney, she was used to working 15-hour days and still finding the energy to run one or two miles most days. She felt absolutely toppled by one little, tiny baby.

You will likely feel incredibly fatigued for the first few days to a week after you deliver your baby. This fatigue is normal and expected. Almost all new moms experience fatigue in the first few days after delivery, and it steadily declines over the first week or two. Fatigue may even be beneficial, as it is your body's way of telling you that you need to rest. It may also help you bond with your infant, as feeling fatigued will make you spend quiet time with your brand-new baby.

Persistent fatigue past two weeks, however, can be highly predictive of the development of postpartum depression. A number of studies have been conducted in this area. One study found that 13 out of 14 women who reported significant fatigue two weeks after delivery had postpartum depression when their baby was one month old. This study has been replicated, and it is clear that fatigue can be an early warning sign that predicts postpartum depression. It is not known, though, whether the fatigue is an early symptom of PPD or whether not getting enough sleep leads to fatigue, which then leads to PPD.

If you are still feeling highly fatigued at two weeks, be sure to get lots more rest and quiet time than you are currently getting. Also, speak to your health care provider about it, to help you and your doctor keep alert for the possibility that you may develop postpartum depression. For more detailed information on postpartum depression and coping with this disorder, see pages 205–18.

Living in a Fog

Katie referred to those days as "The Fuzz." Even years later, she can recall being in an absolute fog the first eight weeks after her daughter was born. "Days and nights became a blur. I felt like a walking zombie

*and couldn't think clearly." But one day she snapped out if it and
began to feel like herself again.*

A common experience of many new moms is feeling like
they are in a fog for the first few weeks to few months. You
will be completely absorbed in taking care of your newborn,
both day and night. The outside world will likely fade away as
you are immersed in feedings, diaper changes, and cuddling
your brand-new baby. In addition, whether it is hormones,
being sleep deprived, getting used to being a new mom, or
just the constant round-the-clock care your newborn requires,
you'll likely feel out of it. You'll feel disconnected from the rest
of the world, whether that means what's happening in world
affairs or just what your best friend has been up to lately.
Forget about your workplace. It all will seem very far away
right now.

Right around the three-month mark, though, the fog will
likely lift. You'll start becoming interested in what's happening
beyond the walls of your home. Some women report that it feels
as if they've come out of hibernation; all of a sudden there is a
whole world out there that matters again.

So How Do You Get Some Sleep?

*Melanie remembered how hard it was when her son was born four
years ago. This time she was better prepared. She told all of her friends
and family that they shouldn't call after 7:00 at night, she hired a
babysitter to come in the afternoon so she could take a nap, and she
asked her mother to stay over one night a week to help out with the
baby so she could catch up on some sleep.*

There are definitely things that you can do to manage these first six weeks to help you not to feel totally sleep deprived. New moms need to be incredibly vigilant about making sleep a priority, as well as establishing and maintaining good sleep habits. You want to maximize your time asleep for those times that you do make it to bed.

- **MAKE SLEEP A PRIORITY.** Be sure that you sleep every chance you get, heading to bed early and lying down when your baby is napping.
- **SLEEP WHEN THE BABY SLEEPS.** The best thing you can do is sleep when your baby sleeps. If your baby naps for an hour at 11:00 in the morning, you should, too. If your baby falls asleep at 9:00 at night, head to bed yourself. Don't stay up to get things done. Remember, you need your sleep more. If you have other children at home, it's going to be a bit more of a balancing act. Hire a babysitter or mother's helper for your older child or children. Or treat your other children to a day away with their favorite person.
- **DEVELOP A RELAXING BEDTIME ROUTINE.** You need a bedtime routine as much as your baby does. Three or four activities that are the same every night and are relaxing, such as a bath, a massage, reading, or listening to relaxing music, make for the best bedtime routine.
- **LEARN TO RELAX.** If you are having a hard time relaxing at bedtime, check out the relaxation exercises that are provided in chapter 7.
- **MAKE YOUR BEDROOM A SLEEP HAVEN.** Ensure that your bedroom is cool, dark, quiet, and comfortable.
- **GET OUTDOORS.** Exposure to bright outdoor light,

especially in the morning, will help both you and your baby sleep better at night.

- **GET EXERCISE.** Exercise at least a few times a week, although nothing too strenuous to start. Even if it's just a short walk around the block or down the street, getting some exercise will give you energy and help you feel better.

- **LIMIT OR AVOID CAFFEINE, NICOTINE, AND ALCOHOL.** All of these will interfere with getting a good night's sleep.

- **EAT WELL.** See pages 199–200 for healthy food choices that you can make to help you feel your best.

- **MANAGE THE OUTSIDE WORLD.** Forget about returning all those phone calls from well-meaning friends and relatives—they'll understand. You should sleep. It will make you a happier person and a better parent. Consider screening your calls with an answering machine or getting caller ID. Discourage drop-in visitors. Your friends and family will eventually have plenty of time with the baby.

- **ASK FOR HELP.** And no matter what, get help. Being a new parent can be overwhelming, and there is no reason to try to do it all yourself. Getting even a half-hour reprieve will make a big difference in your sanity. And friends and family want to help, so let them. In addition, many parents request help only during the day. However, it may be even more beneficial to get help during the night when you are trying to get some sleep. Hire a nanny for nighttime hours instead. Or beg your mother to come spend the night once in a while so that you can get some sleep. You can do this during the day, too, while you take a nap.

- **DEVELOP GOOD SLEEP HABITS FOR YOUR BABY.** To help everyone get a good night's sleep, learn as much as you can about sleep in newborns and infants. Chapter 12 provides all the information that you need to help your baby sleep well. You'll sleep better once your baby is sleeping well. You can start as early as two or three weeks, especially starting to institute a bedtime routine.

Your Newborn's Sleep

HAVING A BABY is one of the most wonderful experiences of a lifetime. Holding this incredible little bundle is absolutely amazing. Unfortunately, that bundle of joy is likely going to keep you up at night, at least to start.

Newborns sleep between 10 and 18 hours a day; however, there is typically no rhyme or reason to their sleep. Your little one may sleep for 30 minutes at a time or 3 hours at a stretch. Also, newborns do not yet differentiate between night and day, so you may have times when your little one is up during the day and sleeping at night, and other times when he's asleep during the day but up all night.

Chapter 12 gives you all the information you need to start getting your baby's sleep on the right track from a very young age. However, this section is more of a warning that you can't expect any predictability for the first 6 to 8 weeks. After that point, your baby will start developing a schedule and will be able to sleep for longer stretches at night.

- **SAVOR THE MOMENTS.** Finally, while it is important to hang in there through those first few weeks with a newborn, be sure to savor the moments. Babies grow so fast, and your baby will never be this tiny again. The time goes by quickly, and the next thing you know, your newborn has become a toddler. As much as time may feel as if it is dragging during those first few weeks when you're pacing the floor with a crying newborn, you will realize later how fast the time really went.

Be Good to Yourself

ALTHOUGH ALL OF your attention is likely focused on your baby, don't forget to take care of yourself. You need to be happy and well rested to be at your best. The better you are to yourself, the better a mom you will be. Some things that you can do to be good to yourself are:

- **GET PLENTY OF REST.** Nap when the baby naps, go to bed early, and sleep in when you can.
- **GET A MANICURE OR A PEDICURE.** You'll now be able to see your toes again, so get a pedicure.
- **GET A MASSAGE.** Many masseuses will even come to your house, which can be the ultimate treat.
- **GO SHOPPING.** You likely still fit only into your maternity clothes, which can be depressing. Splurge on some clothes that make you feel good about yourself, even if you'll only be wearing them for a few months until you lose the baby weight.
- **GET A HAIRCUT.** Splurge and go for the highlights while you are there.
- **READ A LIGHT NOVEL OR MAGAZINE.** Indulge yourself with the latest issue of *People* or *Glamour,* or your favorite author's new book.

- **RENT A MOVIE.** Watch one of the latest movies that you missed at the movie theater. Again, this is not the time to watch some intense movie that grapples with a major social issue. Go for the chick flick!

- **GO EASY ON YOURSELF.** Don't expect that you know everything about parenting and taking care of your little one. This feeling of incompetence can be worrisome, even for moms who have older children. It's amazing how much you'll forget about taking care of a newborn once your older ones are past this stage.

Eating Healthily

CARING FOR A newborn baby can be so time-consuming that your nutrition may suffer. All of a sudden you may realize that you've eaten more fast food in the past few weeks than you've eaten in the last two years! But both you and your baby may not be getting the nutrients you need if you don't take care of yourself. If frozen dinners and pizza have become your staple, here are some other ways to save time and improve your diet:

- **CHOOSE HEALTHY SNACKS.** Healthy snacks will give you more energy and keep you going during the day. Although potato chips and chocolate bars taste great at the moment, they won't sustain you in the long run. Some better choices include:

  - Cheese and crackers
  - Apple slices
  - Almonds
  - Soy nuts
  - Dried fruit (apricots, figs, mango)

- Almond butter on toast
- Peanut butter on pretzels
- Bagel and cream cheese
- Yogurt
- Soy chips
- Flavored rice cakes
- Granola bar
- Snack bar (e.g., Clif, Odwalla)
- Trail mix
- Hard-boiled egg
- Tuna
- Fig Newtons
- Applesauce
- Fresh veggies (precut)
- Rice crackers

- **STOCK UP.** Head to a wholesale store, such as Costco or BJs, and stock up. Fill your freezer with frozen vegetables and ready-to-prepare meals, as well as your cupboard with healthy snacks, such as dried fruit and granola bars.

- **COOKING CLUBS.** Another way to ensure that you are eating better than frozen pizzas and macaroni and cheese is to seek out a local cooking club where you prepare or purchase meals that can be easily prepared. These types of stores and cooking clubs, such as Super Suppers, are popping up all over the country.

- **PRIVATE CHEF.** Private chefs are becoming more and more common these days. Your first reaction is probably, "Oh my, that will be exorbitant," but it actually may not cost as much as you think. It also can be much cheaper than ordering take-out most nights of the week. A private chef does not usually mean a person whom you have hired who cooks only for your family.

Private chefs these days usually take just one day a week or even one day a month and prepare multiple meals for you for the week, or even the month, and store it all with labels in your freezer. By the way, this is a perfect shower or baby gift from friends and family!

Breast-feeding and Sleep

BREAST-FEEDING HAS MANY benefits, and now we can add another to the list—women who exclusively breast-feed get more sleep! Yes, you actually did read that correctly: women who nurse get more sleep. This increase is not only compared to women whose babies are exclusively bottle-fed, but also women who are nursing but supplement with formula in the evening or during the night. Dads also get more sleep when babies are exclusively breast-fed, although that is likely less surprising.

In addition, women who are nursing get more deep sleep. The comparison is rather astounding. In one study, women who were breast-feeding spent 182 minutes of the night in deep sleep, compared to 86 minutes in women who did not have a baby and 63 minutes in women with same age babies who had chosen to bottle-feed their baby. There were no differences in total sleep time or time spent in REM sleep (dreaming sleep) among the three groups. The breast-feeding women spent much less time in stages 1 and 2 of non-REM sleep, which are lighter stages of sleep, spending more time in deep restorative sleep. The reason for this difference is not totally known, but it's probably due to prolactin, a hormone that is vital for breast-feeding. So you may actually get more hours of sleep and more restful sleep if you are nursing!

Nursing, both during the day and at night, has many other positive rewards in addition to sleep benefits. The primary benefit is that breast-feeding is best for babies, but there is also nothing like snuggling with your baby and being that connected. You may even be surprised to find that you miss those bleary nights of nursing at two in the morning. The rest of the world is asleep and it's just you and your baby.

Even if you are exclusively breast-feeding, it doesn't mean that you have to do everything. See page pages 203–04 for helpful hints on how to maximize your sleep, including having someone else give your baby a pumped bottle of breast milk, as well as doing all the other parts of nighttime baby duty, such as diaper changes.

And finally, be sure to pump on the night or two that your baby surprises you and sleeps for a long stretch. You don't want to develop mastitis or be in pain because your body is telling you it's time to nurse while your baby is still fast asleep. Pump enough to take the edge off.

Bottle-Feeding and Sleep

IF YOU ARE bottle-feeding, you are also waking up throughout the night to feed your baby, and it ends up that you may actually be getting less sleep than nursing moms. This is likely due to having to get up and head to the kitchen to get the bottle and heat it up, often while your baby is fussing while waiting to eat. To help you maximize your sleep, prepare plenty of bottles for the night before you head to bed. Some parents find that putting a small refrigerator in the baby's room to store the bottles can save them a trip to the kitchen. There are also portable bottle warmers available that you can keep in your baby's room.

Sharing Nighttime Duty

Lisa and her husband, Stephen, came up with a plan to help both of them get as much sleep as possible when their son Jacob was 3 weeks old. Before that time, no one was getting any sleep, and it didn't seem to make sense for both of them to be up all night. Lisa was breast-feeding, so she would pump at nine at night and head to bed. Stephen would then feed Jacob a bottle of pumped milk around eleven at night and go to bed himself. This system worked well, as Jacob usually didn't wake up until 2:30 for his next feeding. By that point, Lisa had had 5 straight hours of sleep and would then get another 3 or 4 hours of interrupted sleep. Stephen got 6 or 7 hours of uninterrupted sleep, as he didn't have to get up for work until 7:00.

THERE ARE MANY ways that you and your husband (or partner) can share nighttime duty. There is no one right way; you'll need to figure out what works best for your family.

Below are a number of ways to maximize sleep for everyone.

- **SPLIT THE NIGHT.** Some couples completely split night-time duty, with one parent taking the first half of the night and the other parent taking the second half.
- **SWAP NIGHTS.** Another way to share nighttime duty is to switch off who is on baby duty each night. For example, Laurie and Sam literally swapped every other night. Laurie usually took Monday, Wednesday, and Friday nights, and Sam was on Tuesday, Thursday, and Saturday nights. They would flip a coin as to who had to get up with the baby on Sunday nights.
- **SPLIT THE WEEK.** Some couples find it easier to split the week, with one parent on baby duty Sunday through

Wednesday night and the other parent on Thursday through Saturday night.

- **WEEKDAYS VERSUS WEEKENDS.** Even another way is to have one parent responsible for weekday nights and the other for weekend nights. This system works well for couples where one parent is home with the baby and the other works during the week, or for couples where one person's job requires a great deal of traveling during the week.

Realize that when sharing baby duty, whether it's at night or during the day, it doesn't have to be 50–50, with each doing exactly half of the jobs. Sharing can mean lots of different things. For example, Clare was always responsible for the baby, but Dan did his part by doing all the cooking, cleaning, laundry, and grocery shopping. For them, this sharing of household responsibilities worked perfectly.

Nursing Moms and Sharing Nighttime Duty

EVEN MOMS WHO nurse can share nighttime duty. One way is to have someone else give the baby a bottle of pumped milk or formula during the night. If your baby doesn't take bottles, or you prefer to nurse, it can be a huge help if your husband takes care of everything but the feeding in the middle of the night. Have your husband go get the baby and bring her to you, and then he can take the baby afterward for a diaper change and to put her back to bed. This can mean the difference between your being awake for 20 minutes versus being up for 45 minutes or more with each feeding.

Postpartum Depression

Felicia felt like she was always crying. Her baby was 4 days old, and here she was sitting in the bathtub trying to soak her private parts in warm water while at the same time holding bags of frozen peas to her incredibly sore breasts. The baby had slept for much of the time in the hospital, but the moment she came home, she woke up and hadn't slept for more than 30 minutes at a stretch since. Felicia felt incredibly guilty, because all she could think about was whether she had just made the worst mistake of her life by having a baby.

FEELING DEPRESSED IS incredibly common following the birth of a baby. Surprisingly, between 70 and 80 percent of women feel depressed during the first few days after the birth of their baby. This common response is often referred to as the "baby blues." These baby blues usually peak 4 to 5 days after the birth of the baby and last for a week or two. So if you are feeling down, do not be surprised. This is perfectly normal.

Postpartum depression (PPD), a more serious depression, is different from the baby blues in the intensity, frequency, and duration of these feelings. Many women feel sad and anxious at different points during the first few months, whereas women with PPD feel sad and are crying all day long for several days or weeks. Postpartum depression usually starts two to four weeks after the birth of the baby and can last from a few weeks to up to a year. Women with postpartum depression have problems functioning during the day. Even doing the most mundane tasks, like showering and getting dressed, are difficult. They also may worry that they are going to harm their baby or their other children.

It's Not Always Blissful

IT IS IMPORTANT to understand that having a baby is not always blissful. Most women feel ambivalent, angry, sad, or afraid at some point. The desire to return the baby and return to life before your baby's arrival is totally normal, whether this is your first baby or your third. Unfortunately, our society makes it very difficult for women to admit to these feelings. Women are supposed to feel 100 percent positive about being a mom and about their baby. This is just not true and is completely unrealistic. Share your feelings with your husband, your best friend, your mom, or someone else. You'll be surprised at how universal these thoughts are. And definitely do not feel guilty about having these negative feelings!

How Common Is Postpartum Depression?

Postpartum depression is a very common condition. A recent study found that postpartum depression occurs in about 19 percent of women, with an additional 12 percent experiencing major depression within the first year after giving birth. This means that about one-third of all women have some level of postpartum depression, about 500,000 women every year. Postpartum depression typically develops within the first three months, but it can develop even later.

Symptoms of Postpartum Depression

There are a number of possible symptoms of postpartum depression, including the following:

- Sadness throughout the day
- Loss of or diminished interest in formerly enjoyable activities
- Frequent crying
- Insomnia
- Loss of appetite
- Difficulty concentrating
- Decreased energy and motivation
- Irritability
- Moodiness
- Anxiety
- Panic attacks
- Thoughts of harming yourself
- Thoughts of harming your baby
- Feeling that you cannot care for your baby

In very rare cases, a woman can develop postpartum psychosis. This unusual illness is characterized by hallucinations, delusions, bizarre thinking, and sometimes suicidal thoughts. If you develop any symptoms of postpartum psychosis, contact your doctor immediately or go to your local emergency room.

To help you determine whether you may be experiencing postpartum depression, complete the Edinburgh Postnatal Depression Scale. This is a widely used and well-validated measure of PPD.

Quiz

Do You Have Postpartum Depression?:

EDINBURGH POSTNATAL DEPRESSION SCALE

Please choose the answer that comes closest to how you have felt IN THE PAST 7 DAYS, not just how you feel today.

_____ I have been able to laugh and see the funny side of things.

As much as I always could (0)

Not quite so much now (1)

Definitely not so much now (2)

Not at all (3)

_____ I have looked forward and with enjoyment to things.

As much as I ever did (0)

Rather less than I used to (1)

Definitely less than I used to (2)

Hardly at all (3)

_____ I have blamed myself unnecessarily when things went wrong.

Yes, most of the time (3)

Yes, some of the time (2)

Not very often (1)

No, never (0)

_____ I have been anxious or worried for no good reason.

No, not at all (0)

Hardly ever (1)

Yes, sometimes (2)

Yes, very often (3)

_____ I have felt scared or panicky for not very good reason.

Yes, quite a lot (3)

Yes, sometimes (2)

No, not much (1)

No, not at all (0)

_____ Things have been getting on top of me.

Yes, most of the time I haven't been able to cope at all (3)

Yes, sometimes I haven't been coping as well as usual (2)

No, most of the time I have coped quite well (1)

No, I have been coping as well as ever (0)

_____ I have been so unhappy that I have had difficulty sleeping.

Yes, most of the time (3)

Yes, sometimes (2)

Not very often (1)

No, not at all (0)

_____ I have felt sad or miserable.

Yes, most of the time (3)

Yes, quite often (2)

Not very often (1)

No, not at all (0)

_____ I have been so unhappy that I have been crying.

Yes, most of the time (3)

Yes, quite often (2)

Only occasionally (1)

No, never (0)

_____ The thought of harming myself has occurred to me.

Yes, quite often (3)

Sometimes (2)

Hardly ever (1)

Never (0)

SCORING. Add up your score, using the numbers indicated under each answer. Scores can range from 0 to 30.

What does your score mean?

SCORE	
Less than 10	Low likelihood of depression
10 to 12	Possible depression
13 or higher	Likely depression

If your score is 10 or above, or you think that you are depressed but it is not reflected on this questionnaire, be sure to speak to your doctor.

Source: Cox, J. L., Holden, J. M., and Sagovsky, R. (1987). "Detection of postnatal depression: Development of the 10-item Edinburgh Postnatal Depression Scale." *British Journal of Psychiatry 150*, 782–86.

Risk Factors for PPD

There are a number of factors that may put you at higher risk for developing postpartum depression.

- You have a history of depression
- You have a history of postpartum depression

- You are a single mom or your partner is unsupportive
- Your pregnancy was unplanned
- You are having marital problems
- You are having financial problems
- You are experiencing other stressful life events at the same time as having a new baby, such as a move or the loss of a close friend or family member
- You experience severe premenstrual symptoms

Just because you have one or more of these risk factors does not mean, however, that you will definitely develop postpartum depression. It just means that you are more likely to develop PPD. On the other hand, some women develop PPD who have none of these risk factors.

Causes of Postpartum Depression

No one knows for sure what causes postpartum depression, but it is likely caused by multiple physical and emotional factors. First of all, there are many physical changes all occurring at the same time. There is a huge drop in hormone levels immediately after childbirth, with estrogen and progesterone both abruptly dropping after the baby is born. These two hormones affect mood, as you have likely been aware for much of your life (think PMS!). There are also other changes in your body, including changes in blood pressure and metabolism, which affect how you feel. In addition, childbirth itself is labor intensive. Think of running a marathon or doing about a thousand sit-ups at one time. Your body is exhausted. If you had a cesarean section, your body has gone through the added stress of surgery. Add to that chronic sleep deprivation, and it's no surprise that most women feel depressed.

Emotionally, too, there are so many things going on. If this is your first baby, you are likely stunned by both the emotional high of having a baby and the nonstop responsibility. If this is your second, third, or even fourth child, you also have to deal with the demands of your older ones, who are likely extra needy at the moment. Nothing is harder than having an overwrought 2-year-old who is incredibly clingy, not letting you out of his sight so that you can go to the bathroom, while dealing with a fussy newborn.

Relationship Between Sleep Deprivation and PPD

Although, as stated, no one knows for sure what causes postpartum depression, one factor that can be a major contributor is sleep deprivation. As is likely abundantly clear, women with a newborn are not getting as much sleep as they need or would like.

There have been some initial studies that indicate that sleep deprivation can play a role in PPD. One study looked at how moms' fatigue and babies' total sleep time were related to PPD. Not surprisingly, this study found that both are strongly associated with the development of postpartum depression. At one week after childbirth, moms who were not depressed but later developed PPD were more likely to be getting less than six hours of sleep at night, were more tired during the day, and had babies who woke up more at night and cried more often.

So what does this mean for you? One obvious fact reiterated again and again in this book—you need to get sleep! This means either getting your baby to sleep better (see chapter 12) or having someone else take care of the baby for a few hours while you get some rest.

Planning for Postpartum Depression

Rachel, 8 months pregnant, was having an incredibly difficult time just managing her 2-year-old daughter, Mandy. Rachel felt angry much of the time and often lost her patience with Mandy's even smallest transgressions. She was overwhelmed thinking about how she was going to handle Mandy and a newborn, since she knew she could barely handle one child, let alone two. She and her husband were trying to plan ahead. Rachel and her husband decided that she was not going to breast-feed, so that she could go on medication for depression soon after the arrival of the baby. They started Mandy in day care 3 days a week to give everyone a break, and the family started seeing a child psychologist to help the parents learn how to manage Mandy's behavior. They also planned on Rachel's mother coming to stay with them for the first month. Rachel was still feeling overwhelmed, but she felt that they were putting the pieces in place to help the entire family.

It is a good idea to plan ahead for the possibility of feeling depressed. Of course you would rather focus on the excitement of your new baby, but anticipating problems can help prevent them or lessen their impact.

Plan ahead to have extra help around the house, especially during the first few weeks. There are many creative ways to have family and friends be helpful without being intrusive. For example, have your mother or best friend come to help for the first week, but have her stay at a hotel to give your family some alone time. Have a friend or a nanny come for nighttime hours, rather than during the day, if that is when you anticipate needing the most help. Often dinnertime and evenings are the hardest, as that is when the baby is most likely to be fussy and your 3-year-old is at his most demanding. Having an extra pair of hands around from 5:00 to 8:00 p.m. may be the help that you need. There are other things that you can do to help prevent the development of PPD:

- **HAVE YOUR PARTNER SCHEDULE TIME OFF FROM WORK.** Having both parents home during the first week or two can be a tremendous help, especially if you have older children who are going to need attention, too.
- **SEEK OUT SUPPORT GROUPS AND NEW-MOM GROUPS.** Being able to connect with other new moms who are going through a similar experience can be especially helpful.
- **TALK TO YOUR DOCTOR.** It is also important to talk to your doctor now about ways to manage postpartum depression, especially if you are currently feeling depressed or have been depressed in the past. Having a plan will help if the time comes that you need it.

Improving Postpartum Depression

Postpartum depression is highly treatable with counseling and possibly medication. There are also many small things that you can do. First, though, take care of your basic needs—eat well and get plenty of sleep.

- **TAKE TIME FOR YOURSELF.** Even if it's just 10 or 15 minutes each day, take time for yourself. Go soak in the bathtub, call a friend to catch up on the gossip, read a trashy magazine or novel, or just lie down and shut your eyes.
- **SCHEDULE VISITORS.** Visitors can be a wonderful help. Family and friends can keep you company, help with the baby, and make meals. Being able to chat while

folding clean clothes can be a wonderful distraction from those endless loads of laundry.

- **BUT DON'T OVERDO IT.** Visitors are wonderful, but be careful not to overdo it. Too many visitors and social obligations can be exhausting.

- **KEEP A DIARY.** A great deal of research has shown that keeping a diary can be very therapeutic. You will feel better just by journaling and writing down your thoughts.

- **GET REST.** Nap when the baby naps—although that is harder in reality than it sounds. Sleep deprivation is a major contributor to postpartum depression, so be sure to get as much sleep as you can.

- **KEEP YOUR EXPECTATIONS LOW.** Don't make a to-do list that sets you up for failure. There is just no way that in one day you are going to clean the house, run errands, cook dinner, and write up that report for work that you promised at the same time that you are taking care of a demanding little one. You'll feel awful at the end of the day, as you'll focus on all the things that you *didn't* get done. Instead, be realistic. Expect to get just one thing done in a day. That is doable. And feel good about yourself once you have accomplished that one task. On some days, that one task may just be taking a shower and getting dressed!

- **TALK TO SOMEONE.** Call your best friend, your sister, or another new mom. Talk about how you are feeling. Don't try to put on a happy face and present to everyone that life is grand. You need support and you need validation that being a new mom can definitely be tough at times.

- **DON'T FEEL GUILTY ABOUT BEING DEPRESSED.** Feeling depressed does not mean that you are a bad mother or that you do not love your child(ren). You have little control over whether you feel depressed, and it is absolutely no reflection on your parenting.
- **GET OUTDOORS.** Put the baby in a stroller or a front carrier and get outside. Go for a stroll, head to the nearest park, or just sit outside. The bright light will help tremendously, and getting fresh air can be very beneficial, as well as not looking at the same four walls of your home.

Antidepressants for Postpartum Depression

MANY WOMEN TAKE medication for postpartum depression and find it to be extremely beneficial. Whether you decide to take medication is an individual choice. If you are breast-feeding, this is obviously a harder decision. There is no consensus about whether it is safe to take antidepressants while nursing. Some doctors believe that it is fine and others are more cautious. Some women who have severe postpartum depression end up deciding to quit nursing so that they can take an antidepressant. This can be an appropriate decision, especially if you are not functioning. Talk the decision over with your doctor, your husband or partner, and your baby's doctor. Please be reassured that you are not a failure if you make this decision. In some cases, this is the best decision that you can make for your baby.

- **FIND A SUPPORT GROUP.** Many local communities have support groups specifically for women struggling with PPD. Even joining a play group or mom's group can be highly beneficial, especially sharing your thoughts with other women who are going through the exact same experience. An added benefit is that it will get you out of the house.

- **GET HELP FOR YOUR PPD.** Postpartum depression is highly treatable. Talk to your primary doctor, your obstetrician, or a specialist in PPD. Although it may seem as if you'll never feel better, there is help available.

For Dads: Helping Your Wife Deal with PPD

THERE ARE MANY things that you can do to help someone with PPD. Obviously you cannot fix it, but you can provide support. If your wife is suffering from PPD, here are some suggestions that may benefit both of you.

- **DON'T JUDGE.** As hard as it may be, be sure not to judge the person who is dealing with PPD. This especially means not criticizing the way she is caring for the baby. Note that there is a fine line between offering advice and criticizing, and that fine line is even more delicate when the person hearing your advice has PPD.
- **OFFER HELP.** Help in any way that you can. You may need to insist on helping and not just waiting for your wife to request help. One of the best things that you can do is to give your wife a break from the baby. For women with PPD, a trip to the grocery store without the baby can be a huge boon. Honestly, a trip to the bathroom without the baby is greatly appreciated.
- **ENCOURAGE REST.** Encourage your wife to get some rest. This can be during the day and/or at night. Helping your wife get some sleep can help ease the depression symptoms. Even

if she doesn't sleep, just taking some time to lie down and rest can help.

- **LISTEN.** Listen to your wife's concerns and take her seriously.
- **TELL YOUR WIFE THAT YOU LOVE HER.** Your wife is likely feeling at her worst. Reassure her that you still love her and think she is wonderful. Provide extra hugs, bring home her favorite chocolates, and leave her a note in the morning telling her that you love her. It's often the little things that mean the most.
- **HELP YOUR WIFE SEEK TREATMENT.** Encourage your wife to talk to her obstetrician or doctor to get treatment. If you can, go along with her to her appointment so that you can learn as much as you can about PPD and help your wife evaluate her treatment options.

Reminders

- Be sure to sleep when you can! There are many things that you can do to get more sleep, including sleeping when the baby sleeps, getting outdoors, getting exercise, asking for help, and learning about newborn and infant sleep.
- Don't be surprised if you are especially tired and feel as if you are in a fog during the first few weeks after your baby is born.
- Be good to yourself. Eat healthily, splurge on a massage or a pedicure, go shopping, read a fun book, and don't put pressure on yourself to know everything and be the perfect parent.

- Breast-feeding actually leads to more sleep for new moms. Also, share nighttime duty to help everyone get the sleep they need.
- Postpartum depression affects almost 20 percent of new moms. Talk to your doctor if you think you may be having problems with PPD. There is help available.

ELEVEN

Six Weeks to Six Months

"Help! Will I ever get a good night's sleep again?"
—*Becca, mom of a 2-month-old*

"I'm so tired that I feel like crying all the time."
—*Elizabeth, mom of a 5-month-old*

Now that you are past the early newborn period, your baby will start to be more predictable and you'll be feeling more and more like yourself. However, don't be surprised if your sleep has still not returned to normal. For the majority of new moms it can take a long time—six months, or even a year or two after their baby is born. The National Sleep Foundation's *Sleep in America Poll 2007* found that 60 percent of new moms (3 out of 5 women) report that they are not sleeping as well as before they were pregnant. For those whose sleep has returned to normal, this occurred anytime between when their baby was 2 weeks and 6 months old. For example, 6 percent of women said that they were sleeping well again within the first two weeks (hard to believe), and 10 percent reported that it took 12 or more weeks to get back to normal.

How quickly your sleep returns to normal has much to do, obviously, with how well your baby sleeps. Beyond your baby's influence, though, it may still take awhile for you to adjust. One thing that can be very frustrating is to still be waking up at night well after your baby is sleeping through the night. Some of these sleep issues may be related to sleep problems that existed before you were pregnant, but primarily it is because it can take awhile to get back into your own rhythm. You may be waking up a number of times during the night anticipating that your baby is about to wake up. You may worry when your baby doesn't wake up, wondering if there is something wrong.

The first night Andrea's 4-month-old slept through the night, Andrea still woke up three times. The baby was sleeping peacefully, but she wasn't.

"Babies Are Naturally Born Sleep Disorders"

I RECENTLY HEARD someone make this statement and it is a classic. Babies are just that—naturally born sleep disorders.

Moms and Sleep by the Numbers

THERE HAVE BEEN several recent polls regarding sleep in moms. As you would expect, most moms of infants are not getting the sleep that they need. The National Sleep Foundation's *Sleep in America Poll 2004* found that moms of infants are awakened an average of four nights a week, losing close to an hour of sleep each time. That's more than 100 hours of lost sleep in their child's first six months. Think about it—that's almost two weeks worth of sleep!

Other polls of moms have also found that they are not getting enough sleep, with half of all moms thinking they would be better parents if they could get more sleep. Sleep problems are also common. The recent National Sleep Foundation's *Sleep in America Poll 2007* found that 84 percent of postpartum women (with babies under 6 months) experience insomnia, and 42 percent report that they rarely or never get a good night's sleep. Twenty percent (one out of five) have even driven drowsy with their child in the car.

How to Get More Sleep and Feel Less Sleep Deprived

THERE ARE A number of small changes that you can make that will make it possible for you to get more sleep, or at least some rest. Resting may not be as totally rejuvenating as actually sleeping, but it can help tremendously. Even just picking one or two of these can make a world of difference in how you feel.

- **NAP WHEN THE BABY NAPS.** Everyone always says to nap when the baby naps, but for a lot of moms, that is hard to do. It's a lot of pressure to immediately fall asleep when your baby does. Instead, go for resting, and if you fall asleep, even better. Turn off the phone, ignore all the e-mails that are piling up, and lie down in a quiet, dark room.
- **GET SOMEONE TO WATCH THE BABY WHILE YOU NAP.** There isn't a rule that says that you must leave the house when you have a babysitter or another person in to help. Ask a relative, a friend, or a babysitter to watch the baby, and go take a nap.
- **CHANGE YOUR PRIORITIES.** With a brand-new little one in the house, this is not the time to worry about a sparkling clean house, gourmet meals on the table,

a front garden worthy of being showcased in a home magazine, or being perfectly made up. Instead, go for easy, nutritious foods, let the dusting go, and forget the mascara.

- **SPLURGE A BIT.** Especially for the first six months or so, it may be hugely beneficial to splurge a bit on things that you normally do yourself. Hire someone to come and clean your house, get a garden service to mow your lawn, or pay to have your groceries delivered after ordering them online. Just taking away one or two demands from your daily or weekly life can make a huge difference.

- **STEP AWAY FROM ALL THE CAFFEINE.** Having a cup of coffee, tea, or your favorite caffeinated beverage is fine for a morning pick-me-up, but avoid getting into the habit of drinking it throughout the day to stay awake. It can develop into a vicious cycle, with the caffeine keeping you up at night followed by feeling lousy again the next day.

- **GO TO BED EARLY.** With a newborn or young infant at home, head to bed early. So what if you haven't gone to bed at 8:00 or 9:00 since you were a kid—go to bed! Knowing that the baby will likely be up during the night, get your sleep when you can, even if that means heading to bed before the sun sets in the summer months.

- **DURING THE NIGHT, LIE DOWN WHILE NURSING OR FEEDING YOUR BABY.** Just being able to lie down instead of sitting up can help you feel a bit more rested during nighttime feedings.

- **DECIDE WHERE THE BABY SHOULD SLEEP AT NIGHT.** Some parents find it helpful to have their baby sleep in a crib or a bassinet in their room at night. This can decrease nightly trips down the hall when the baby wakes up for a feeding. Some parents, though, find that they get less sleep with the baby nearby, as they hear every little grunt and movement. Figure out what works best in your family to ensure that everyone is getting as much sleep as possible.

"Put on Your Own Oxygen Mask Before Helping Others"

IF YOU HAVE flown, you have probably heard this airline safety message. A similar message could be given about sleep. Although you may feel that you need to be available to your baby every hour of the day, don't forget that you have needs, too. One of those needs is sleep. If you push yourself to the point of exhaustion, you are not going to be any help to your baby or to anyone else. You have to take care of yourself so that you can take care of your baby. So don't feel that it's selfish to head to bed and hand over baby duty to someone else. It's actually doing the right thing.

- **TURN OFF THE MONITOR.** If you can hear your baby from your bedroom, which most parents can, then turn off the baby monitor! You need to hear when your baby is upset and needs you, not every breath that she takes. This is especially true with video monitors. You'll be so distracted watching your baby all night long that you'll never get any sleep.
- **TAKE A NIGHT OFF.** Take just one night to catch up on your sleep. Get Dad, Grandma, Nanny, or your best friend to take care of the baby while you get one night of sleep. This may mean that you need to sleep away

from home, whether it's heading to your own parents'
home or even to a hotel. If you are nursing, pump
before and while you're away and your baby can take
bottles of pumped milk.

- **BE PREPARED FOR THOSE NIGHTTIME WAKINGS.** If your
  baby is going to be up for a diaper change or a feeding during the night, have everything prepared. Prefill
  bottles if your baby is taking formula. Have the diaper
  and wipes out on the changing table rather than rum-
  maging looking for everything you need during the
  wee hours of the night.
- **INSTALL DIMMERS.** Light will wake up your brain and
  make it harder to fall back asleep during the night. So
  install dimmer switches in your bathroom, your bedroom, and your baby's bedroom.

Develop a Schedule

Once your baby is 6 to 8 weeks old, starting a daily schedule
is critical. You are likely at the point where gaining some predictability will be welcome, and babies are now physiologically
ready for a schedule. They are starting to produce melatonin,
the hormone that governs our internal clocks. One study found
that babies begin to consolidate their sleep and develop a sleep
schedule once they are 46 weeks post-conception, right around
4 to 8 weeks after birth for full-term babies. Finally, babies
thrive on routine. Having consistency every day will lead to a
happier and calmer baby.

So where do you begin? One place to start is with your baby's
feedings, scheduling them to occur at regular times during the
day. For example, if your baby usually eats every 3 to 4 hours,
set a schedule of every 3 hours (6:00 a.m., 9:00 a.m., noon,

3:00 p.m., 6:00 p.m., and bedtime at 8:00 p.m.). Your baby will be ready to eat at each of these feeding times but won't be starving. If your baby gets hungry in between feedings, of course feed her, but then feed her again at her next scheduled feeding. This type of schedule will balance both demand feedings and maintaining a schedule. Once you know when your baby is usually going to eat, you'll have a better sense of your day.

In addition, institute a sleep schedule. To start, figure out your baby's usual wake time. If she is not awake at that time, then wake her (yes, wake your baby). The time that your baby wakes up for the day actually sets the day's schedule. You can do the same with naps. Decide when your baby is going to nap, and then wake her at her usual wake time if she's not up yet. For example, if she usually naps from 9:30 a.m. to 11:00, then wake her by 11:15 at the latest. Do the same for all of her naps, whether she naps at set times or naps after being awake for two hours. You are basically waking your baby just so she'll be ready to sleep again later, but it works well.

Finally, it is best to institute a feed-play-sleep schedule. That is, feed your baby when she first wakes up, and then have playtime, followed by her next nap or bedtime.

Accept Chaos

Wendy either had to laugh or cry. She chose laughter, as she didn't think tears were going to help the situation. She had a major deadline at work, was up several times during the night with 5-month-old Madison, and woke up that morning to several inches of snow on the ground. Of course her husband was out of town, so it was up to her to get the baby and their 2-year-old up and dressed, shovel something of a path to her car, and get everyone out the door by 7:30. Just as she thought she had everything under control, with both kids buckled into

their car seats, her 2-year-old announced, "My tummy feels funny,"
and promptly threw up all over the three of them.

You might as well just accept it. From now on, there will always be at least some level of chaos in your life. Part of being a mom is learning to multitask and accepting that everything won't always be under your control and everything won't always go exactly as you planned.

Although it is very difficult, try to see the humor in situations as much as you can. Tell yourself that at some point it will make a great story, and realize that you can't always control everything and just need to go with the flow.

Remember, there is no such thing as being a perfect parent! You cannot meet your baby's and family's every single need, every single time. It is literally not possible. You also can't stay calm and patient every single moment of every single day, although that is the way perfect moms are often depicted in the media. You will have moments when you will lose your cool. At those times, it is best to walk away from the situation, count to 10, and take a deep breath. Your baby will be fine in her crib or someplace else safe while you get your emotions under control.

You also can't always be the perfect homemaker. Don't expect to always maintain a home that is exquisitely decorated for every holiday, have flowers beautifully planted in your front yard that change with the season, or design the ultimate birthday party. Nor is being a mom about striving to meet someone else's ideal. You don't have to puree all your own baby food, play Mozart to expose your baby to classical music from day one, or never put on a video for your toddler so you can have a few moments of peace and quiet.

Being a parent isn't always fun—and that's okay. Parenting is likely one of the hardest things you'll ever do. There will be plenty of days when parenting feels like drudgery and you will wonder if it's worth it. There will even be days when you're not even sure if you like your child. That is all part of being a parent. Ask any mom, and if she's candid, she'll let you know that she can't do it all either. So accept help, relax, and enjoy the kind of mom that you are able to be.

Get Exercise

> Joanne lived on the sixth floor in her apartment building. She was tired of feeling flabby and out of shape after the birth of her daughter, Jessica. She began by walking down to the fifth floor and taking the elevator from there. After a week, she began getting off at the fifth floor and taking the stairs for the last flight up. Within a few weeks, she was walking down three flights and walking up two. She couldn't believe how quickly she saw an improvement in her leg and stomach muscles.

Exercise can make a huge difference in how you feel and how much energy you have. We all hate to admit it, but most of us are not back to our prior svelte (or not-so-svelte) self since the baby was born. In addition, it's hard to find time to exercise when you are home with a baby. Now that you are past the newborn stage, add exercise to your day.

Getting exercise, however, doesn't mean having to go to a gym three or four times a week for an hour. That may just be impossible with a brand-new baby. There are simple ways, though, that you can get some exercise, even if it's just a small amount. A small amount is definitely better than nothing.

- **TAKE A WALK.** Put your baby in the stroller and get outside, even if it's just for a walk around the block.

Going for a walk will not only get your body moving but you'll also feel better getting out of your house or apartment.

- **PARK FARTHER AWAY.** It is so tempting to park in the closest spot that you can find when heading to the store or to the doctor's office. Instead, find a parking spot that is one of the farthest away. Those few extra steps can make a big difference.
- **TAKE THE STAIRS.** If you live in an apartment building or work in a building with more than one floor, take the stairs. You can start slow by just taking the stairs down. Then start taking the stairs going up, beginning with just one flight.
- **WEAR A PEDOMETER.** Wear a pedometer to see how many steps you take on an average day. After a week, see if you can beat that number. By keeping track of how far you go every day, you'll be motivated to walk more.
- **WANDER THE MALL.** Head to any mall in the middle of the day, and you'll see plenty of moms pushing strollers. Rather than lie on your couch with the baby and eat potato chips, walk the mall to get some exercise. Sure, it would be best if you got on the treadmill for 30 minutes, but the likelihood of that happening is low. Instead, realize that exercise is exercise and walking around the mall for an hour can be a good choice.
- **DANCE WITH YOUR BABY.** Dancing with your baby is a great deal of fun and will get you some exercise. Whether you decide to samba, tango, rock 'n' roll, or just plain ol' boogie around the living room, the music will get you up and moving. Dancing with your baby will also bring a smile to your face and your baby's.

- **EXERCISE WITH YOUR BABY.** There are many exercises that you can do while interacting with your baby. Playing "horsey" with your baby (have her sit on your feet and bounce your legs) makes for great leg lifts. Strengthen your arms by lifting your baby as if she were a hand weight. Run up and down the stairs with your baby in a front pack (just as effective as a Stairmaster!).

Dads Need Sleep, Too!

NOT ONLY DO moms not get enough sleep, but neither do dads. Studies show that dads get about a half hour less sleep at night after the baby is born. They wake more often at night and for longer.

But it's not a competition. A recent poll of moms and dads found that almost half of new parents argue over who gets less sleep. This led to the coining of the term "competitive sleep syndrome." This is a competition that you want to lose, and one that you don't want to have in the first place. Develop strategies so that everyone shares the burden of nighttime duty and everyone gets as much sleep as possible.

Still Can't Sleep?

Yvonne was exhausted by the end of the day. Taking care of three children under the age of 5 was enough to tire anyone out. However, once she finally got into bed, she couldn't fall asleep. Part of the problem was that she was anxious that at any moment her 4-month-old was going to wake up.

Many new moms have a hard time sleeping, even after instituting good sleep habits. Part of it, as discussed above, can be related to taking awhile to get back on track, but other sleep problems can develop or continue from prepregnancy days. Be sure to read chapters 7 through 9 to review the most common sleep disorders, including insomnia, restless legs syndrome, periodic limb movement disorder, and obstructive sleep apnea.

Sleeping Pills and Nursing

TAKING ANY MEDICATION is a concern for nursing moms. The following information is what is known about specific medications approved for the treatment of insomnia while nursing.

- **BENADRYL (DIPHENHYDRAMINE):** Infants are especially sensitive to the effects of antihistamines, and side effects could occur in a breast-feeding baby.
- **AMBIEN (ZOLPIDEM):** Zolpidem does pass into breast milk and may affect a nursing baby.
- **SONATA (ZALEPLON):** Zaleplon does pass into breast milk and may affect a nursing baby.
- **LUNESTA (ESZOPICLONE):** Eszopiclone does pass into breast milk and may affect a nursing baby.
- **ROZEREM (RAMELTEON):** It is unknown if ramelteon passes into breast milk.

Do not take any of these medications if you are nursing without first talking to your doctor.

Going Back to Work

GOING BACK TO work after having a baby can be very stressful. Maybe you're heading back to work only because you have no choice financially, or maybe you're relieved to be returning, but no matter what your reason, you will likely have a difficult time leaving your baby. And whether you are dreading it or are thrilled, getting some sleep is going to be crucial.

WHAT YOU CAN DO. There are a number of things that you can do to manage when it's time to head back to work.

- **EVALUATE YOUR WORK OPTIONS.** Find out whether or not your employer offers alternative work schedules, such as flex hours, a compressed work week, or job sharing. See if you can telecommute one or two days a week. Even if your workplace has never done so in the past, that doesn't mean they won't do so now. Having flexibility can greatly reduce your job stress and help you balance your family's needs.

- **FIND GOOD CHILD CARE.** The hardest part about returning to work for most women is worrying about their baby. Find good quality child care that you feel comfortable with, whether that is a nanny in your home, a neighbor who watches children in her home, or a child care center. These days more and more fathers are staying at home while the wife returns to work. Explore your options and decide what works best for your family.

- **ROUTINE, ROUTINE, ROUTINE.** Households that function at their best are ones in which there are consistent routines every day. This of course includes bedtime routines, but there are others. For example, develop a routine for getting up and ready in the morning. Your day may start with cuddle time while nursing, followed by taking a shower while the baby is in a swing. Have a routine, too, for what happens when you get home from work. The more routines you have in place, the less you'll experience chaos and the more your baby will know what to expect.

- **GET ORGANIZED.** The more organized that you are, the less time you will waste and the more you will feel in control. For example, every day when you get home from work go through your baby's diaper bag and refill it with all the things that are needed for the next day, such as diapers, wipes, and spare clothing. Always put your keys and your purse in exactly the same place when you get home, so there is no more frantic searching. Figuring out an organizational system may take some work, but it will pay off greatly.

- **GET EVERYONE TO BED EARLY.** Although it is very tempting to keep your baby up when you get home from work so that you can spend time together, everyone will be happier if you set an early bedtime. Your baby needs sleep and so do you. Keeping your baby up past her bedtime can result in one cranky and unhappy baby. Instead, head to bed and enjoy your waking hours together.

- **GETTING SLEEP WILL HELP YOU BE MORE EFFICIENT AND GET MORE DONE.** Counter to what you might expect, you will actually be more efficient and get more done if you get eight hours of sleep every night. Your brain will be more alert and process information quicker. You'll also have the energy to get things done, so you'll accomplish more in less time.

- **TURN OFF THE WORLD IN THE EVENING.** Everyone needs some downtime in the evenings, especially before heading to bed. If your evenings are spent calling friends and checking e-mail, you will all of a sudden find that it is 10:00 at night and you haven't had a moment to unwind. Instead, turn off the world. Send your phone to voice mail or just don't answer it. Turn off your computer and wait until the next day to check your e-mail.

- **DEVELOP GOOD SLEEP HABITS.** Chapter 3 provides lots of information on ways to help you get a good night's sleep. Review these to be sure you are maintaining good sleep habits.

- **DON'T FEEL GUILTY ABOUT MAKING CHANGES TO YOUR CHILD'S SLEEP.** Many working moms feel bad that they are not with their child all day, and so make allowances at night. By inadvertently supporting your baby's poor sleep habits, such as going in and rocking him to sleep every night and throughout the night, you will end up with both you and your child not getting the sleep that you both need. Instead, you are both actually better off if you make changes to help your baby sleep through the night. Not only will you feel better and be a better mom, but your child will feel better, too. Your 6-month-old feels just as crummy waking up twice during the night as you do!

- **DON'T FEEL GUILTY ABOUT WORKING.** Some women feel guilty in the morning when they are leaving their baby to go to work. On the other hand, some women feel guilty at the end of the day leaving work to care for their child. And some women feel guilty at both times.

Don't (although it's easier said than done). It is fine to have both a family and a job!

- **PROTECT YOUR DAYS OFF.** As tempting as it may be, take some downtime on your days off. Don't spend your entire weekend or days off running around doing errands. Days off are meant to be days off—time to relax and recharge.

- **MANAGE YOUR TIME.** Figure out ways to be more efficient to gain yourself some extra time. Cook several meals at once, serving one of those meals and freezing the rest for the days when you don't have time to cook. When out running errands, get several things accomplished rather than heading out on several occasions. Go through mail or e-mails just once, responding to each of them as they come in. Don't waste time rereading e-mails or trying to write the perfect response.

- **KEEP LISTS.** Keep daily lists of things that you need to accomplish for both home and work. Crossing each item off your list will help you feel as if you are getting things accomplished. In addition, you won't waste time and energy trying to remember everything that you need to get done. Be realistic, though, in your list making. Make to-do lists that can actually get accomplished, rather than overzealous and unrealistic lists that will make you feel that you are constantly behind or a failure.

Coping with Feeling Sleep Deprived at Work

There is no question that there will be days (or nights if you are a shift worker) that you will head to work exhausted. Even if your baby is a perfect sleeper, there will be nights when he gets up, whether he's sick, teething, or just looking for a little cuddle time. There are some things that you can do to help you function during the day when you are sleep deprived.

- **CONSIDER A CUP OF COFFEE.** Although too much caffeine can end up interfering with sleep, caffeine can be a safe way to give you an energy boost during the day. It is much better to use caffeine in the morning, though, as late afternoon or evening caffeine may make it hard for you to fall asleep at night, perpetuating your feeling badly during the day. If you are nursing, be sure to speak to your doctor about how much caffeine is safe for you to have. See pages 42–43 for amounts of caffeine in various foods and beverages.
- **SAVE MUNDANE TASKS FOR DOWNTIMES.** Rather than waste your most energetic period during the day on mundane tasks, save those tasks for times in the day when your energy is low. Clean off your desk, return easy phone calls, and go through your e-mails when you are at your sleepiest. The added bonus of relegating some of these tasks to certain periods of the day is that people will realize that you only respond to e-mails or return phone calls at those times, leaving you uninterrupted times to get things done.
- **DO YOUR MOST IMPORTANT TASKS WHEN YOU HAVE THE ENERGY.** And the codicil to the suggestion above is to do the most important things when you have the most energy. This may mean scheduling important meetings or doing concentrated writing first thing in the morning, or whenever is your best time of the day.
- **TAKE A BRIEF NAP.** More and more workplaces are developing policies that allow workers to take a short

nap! Take a 15-minute nap if your job allows it. It can make the world of difference in taking the edge off your sleepiness.

- **KEEP HEALTHY SNACKS AT WORK.** Have a stash of granola bars or dried fruit at work to perk you up when you are feeling exhausted.
- **TAKE A STROLL.** If you are starting to fall asleep at your desk, get up, stretch, and take a walk. Even something this simple can be rejuvenating.

Don't Forget Your Marriage

ONCE THE BLUR of the first few weeks has passed and you're starting to feel like you are getting back to normal, don't forget your marriage or relationship. Stay connected with your partner. The first few years of parenthood are known to be stressful on marriages, a time when many divorces occur. So focus some energy and attention on your marriage. Although you may not feel that there is enough time in the day and you are just too tired, you will feel better taking a moment to stay connected. As you'll notice, there are many little things that you can do that can make a big difference.

- **STAY CONNECTED.** Don't just rely on your friends and family for support; communicate with your spouse. The more you share about how you are feeling, the stronger your relationship. Staying connected doesn't have to mean having intense and meaningful talks. A quick chat can do the trick. Send an e-mail a couple of times a day if a phone call isn't possible. Take ten minutes at the end of the day, once the baby is asleep, to reconnect. Share small moments from your day. Catch each other up on the day's gossip or a funny story about the baby.

- **DO SOMETHING POSITIVE FOR YOUR SPOUSE.** Doing something nice doesn't mean having to do something big. It's usually the small things that really matter. Have a cup of coffee waiting for him when he gets out of the shower. Slip a note into his jacket pocket once in a while. Send a free e-card out of the blue. Or do one of his chores unexpectedly, such as taking out the garbage or making the bed.

- **HAVE FUN.** Sometimes parents get so caught up in day-to-day life that they forget to have fun. Do something enjoyable with your spouse. Go for a drive, have a picnic in the backyard, or go bowling. Even enjoying your baby's antics and laughing together will keep you feeling like a team and a family.

- **SPEND TIME TOGETHER.** When life is busy, it's often tough to find time to do something together. Spending time together doesn't have to be scheduling a date for dinner and a movie. This may not be realistic with a new baby, especially if you don't have family or friends nearby to babysit. You can spend time together in little ways. Go grocery shopping together. Pick up fast food together and simply sit in the car and eat it in the parking lot. There won't be any distractions from the outside world, and you can both grab a quick bite and spend a few minutes together.

- **BEGIN BUILDING YOUR OWN FAMILY TRADITIONS.** You probably recall your favorite family traditions, whether it's the waffles that your own dad always made for breakfast on Sunday mornings, decorating Christmas cookies with your grandmother, or family movie night every Friday. Although your baby is still very young, you can start building your own family traditions. These traditions may be as simple as everyone snuggling in bed on Sunday mornings or singing the same silly bedtime song every night. Building your own family traditions will help you connect with your husband or partner and strengthen the bonds in your newly developing family.

Realize That Nothing Is Forever

TIME SEEMS TO have a different meaning for moms during a baby's first year. For some reason, time gets distorted and everything feels as if it will be this way forever. If you have a 7-year-old who has been having problems sleeping for the past week, you'll perceive it as a stage, a blip on the radar screen. If your 7-month-old has similar problems, you'll feel like she's been having problems "forever" and it will never change. Instead, take a step back and realize that a week or two weeks is just that; your child will keep growing, and things will improve.

Reminders

- New moms are not getting the sleep they need. To help you get more sleep and be more rested, be sure to take care of yourself, don't worry about being the perfect homemaker, and accept a little chaos in your life.
- Exercise can be extremely beneficial in the way you feel (and the way you look).

- If you are heading back to work, there are things that you can do to manage work and being a mom. Evaluate your work options, get super-organized, and manage your time.
- Don't forget to focus some time and energy on your marriage. Stay connected and develop your own family traditions.

TWELVE

Helping Your Baby Sleep Through the Night

"Alicia is 8 weeks old and I'm exhausted. Will she ever sleep for more than four hours at a time?"
—*Lauren*

"Owen is 5 months old and still wakes up twice at night. All I need to do is pop his pacifier back in his mouth. Should I take it away completely?"
—*Sharon*

You've brought home your brand-new baby. Of course, you don't expect him to be sleeping through the night right from the start. But what can you expect when it comes to sleep? First, know that almost all babies do not sleep for extended periods of time for the first 6 to 8 weeks of life. However, starting at about this time, there are things that you can do to get your baby to begin to sleep for longer stretches and start sleeping through the night.

How much sleep do infants need? To learn about how much sleep young children are actually getting, we collected data on over 5,000 infants and toddlers in the United States and Canada. Below are the actual hours of sleep that babies are getting. (Note that this may not reflect actual need, as some babies may actually need more sleep than they are getting.)

	0 to 3 months	3 to 6 months
Total hours of sleep in a 24-hour day	13.3 hours *(range = >9 to <18)*	12.3 hours *(range = >9 to <15)*
Total hours of sleep at night	7.5 hours *(range = >5 to <10)*	8.5 hours *(range = >6.5 to <10)*
Total hours of sleep during the day	5.8 hours *(range = >3 to <9)*	3.8 hours *(range = >2 to <6)*
Number of night wakings	1.9 times *(range = 0 to 5)*	1.2 times *(range = 0 to 5)*
Total time awake during the night	72 minutes *(range = 0 to 130)*	30 minutes *(range = 0 to 70)*
Number of naps	3.6 naps	2.9 naps

In this chapter, you'll find information on ways to manage your infant's sleep. Establishing good sleep habits for your baby early on will ensure that she starts sleeping through the night sooner and will help everyone get the sleep they need!

Be Realistic

At first her baby's sleep patterns drove Sue crazy. Owen, her 6-month-old, would nap for just 45 minutes at a time. She tried everything to get him to nap longer, but nothing seemed to work. She felt as if she was spending all day trying to get him to sleep. Once she realized that there really was a pattern to his sleep, napping for 45 minutes and then awake for 2 hours, she relaxed and realized that this was just his way.

WHEN IT COMES to your baby's sleep, you need to have realistic expectations. Although your baby may turn out to sleep well, don't expect him to in the first 3 months of life. For some babies, this may even be the first 6 months. Newborns just aren't great sleepers and their sleep is not predictable.

EVERY BABY IS DIFFERENT. Don't bother comparing your first-born and your second-born, or comparing your baby to your best friend's baby. Every baby is different and each will have a different sleep pattern. Some babies need more sleep than others. Some are early birds, waking every morning at 5:30; others are inherently little night owls. And finally, no matter what you do, some babies are going to be champion sleepers, while others are going to need every bit of help they can get to keep them on track to sleep well during the day and throughout the night.

BABIES NEED FEEDINGS. Since your infant will need nighttime feedings, this means that you cannot expect your 2- or 3-month-old to sleep for 10 to 12 hours straight. However, most babies no longer need nighttime feedings after 6 months of age, unless there is a growth concern. Note that there are some babies who begin to sleep for long stretches from a very early age, but remember that every baby is different.

WEIGHT HAS NOTHING TO DO WITH SLEEP. There is an old wives' tale that states that once a baby weighs 12 pounds, she is able to sleep through the night. Others say 10 pounds—but it's just not true. Many studies have been done, and every single one has found that how much a baby weighs has nothing to do with how long she can sleep at night.

BABIES COME AS DIFFERENT KINDS OF NAPPERS. Moms often think that the "right" nap schedule is one in which their baby takes a fairly long morning nap and a second, fairly long afternoon nap. Many babies do nap according to this schedule, napping every day around 9:00 a.m. and 2:00 p.m. for an hour and a half or more. But there are many babies who do not.

The second group of babies usually takes 3 or 4 shorter naps throughout the day, usually 30 to 45 minutes long. And they are fine! This is just their natural rhythm. For these babies, their naps are usually interspersed with two hours of being awake. (This is known as the "2-hour rule"—your baby will be ready to take a nap *exactly* two hours after she last woke up.)

And a warning: some babies continue with several short naps throughout the day for a long time, even up to 9 or 10 months of age. Moms often find this schedule frustrating, as all their friends have more predictable days and everyone else's babies seem to sleep for long periods. Some moms also feel that their baby is not the "same" as other babies. But be assured. Your baby is totally fine and this is just her style.

ONCE A GOOD SLEEPER MAY NOT ALWAYS BE A GOOD SLEEPER.
Even the absolute best sleeper is going to have nights when she wakes up. This may occur after being sick, after a trip, or for no apparent reason. Don't be alarmed by a few difficult nights. Stick with what you have always done and your baby will get back on track.

Sleep Safety

BEFORE YOU BEGIN to think about how to get your baby to be a good sleeper and sleep through the night, be sure to consider safety. Below is information on reducing the risk of sudden infant death syndrome (SIDS) and ensuring that your baby has a safe place to sleep at night.

Reduce the Risk of SIDS

Sudden infant death syndrome (SIDS) is a tragic event when a baby dies for no known reason. These deaths typically occur while a baby is sleeping. Unfortunately, we don't know of a way to prevent SIDS completely. The following recommendations, however, will help reduce your baby's risk of being a victim of SIDS.

SLEEP POSITION. First, have your young infant sleep on his or her back. Babies who sleep on their stomachs are more susceptible to SIDS. In the past, pediatricians in the United States recommended that babies sleep on their stomachs or sides because there were concerns that babies may choke if they vomit while asleep on their backs. New research indicates that this is highly unlikely. In contrast, studies have found a significant decrease in SIDS in babies who sleep on their back; in fact, this is the basis of the national campaign called "Back to Sleep," which informs parents that this is the preferred sleep position for babies. This campaign has been highly successful and has reduced the incidence of SIDS by almost 50 percent. Not only has "Back to Sleep" been launched in the United States, but it has also been instituted worldwide with great success.

At some point your baby may decide that he wants to sleep on his stomach and will keep rolling into this position throughout the night. Most babies who are able to roll over onto their stomachs are past the high-risk SIDS period. Speak with your pediatrician if this happens to be sure that your baby is not at risk for SIDS. With your pediatrician's approval, it's okay for your baby to sleep this way.

AVOID BED SHARING. In October 2005 the American Academy of Pediatrics issued a statement recommending that families avoid bed sharing, as this increases the risk of SIDS. There are a number of potential reasons why sharing a bed with your baby can increase her risk of SIDS, including overheating your baby with your body heat (see below), accidentally suffocating or smothering your baby, and also from increased carbon dioxide that may accumulate from your breathing. It is better to use a sidecar sleeper (a bassinet that attaches to the side of your bed) if you wish to have your baby nearby during the night.

PACIFIERS. Interestingly, there is some initial data that indicate that pacifier use decreases the risk for SIDS. If your baby has no interest in a pacifier, obviously you do not want to force its use. However, this appears to be a benefit of pacifiers beyond being just soothing to babies.

STOP SMOKING AROUND YOUR BABY. Studies have shown that mothers who smoke throughout pregnancy and following the birth of their baby triple the risk of their baby's dying from SIDS. Some women quit smoking during pregnancy but return to smoking once the baby is born. These babies are at twice the risk for SIDS. You should never smoke, or let others smoke, near your baby.

USE FIRM BEDDING. Babies should sleep on a firm, flat mattress. Babies should not sleep on beanbag cushions, sheepskins, foam pads, quilts, pillows, or any other soft item. These soft items can be dangerous because your baby can easily smother. Also avoid having your baby sleep on a waterbed, sofa, or any other soft surface.

AVOID OVERHEATING YOUR BABY. SIDS has been associated with babies who are overheated by too much clothing, too many blankets, or too warm a room. This is especially true for a baby with a cold or infection. You can tell if your baby is overheated by whether she is sweating, or has damp hair, a heat rash, or rapid breathing. Dress your baby in as much or as little clothing as you are wearing to sleep. It is also best to dress your baby in nighttime clothing so that no other blankets or other coverings are necessary, such as a footed blanket sleeper during the winter months. Finally, keep bedrooms at a consistent 68 to 70 degrees Fahrenheit.

Crib Safety

A significant number of children are injured, and even killed, in crib accidents. Every year, there are approximately 11,500 crib-related injuries that require hospital treatment. The U.S. Consumer Product Safety Commission estimates that approximately 30 children die each year in unsafe cribs (typically older, previously used cribs). Prior to the institution of current crib standards, there were 200 to 250 deaths a year.

To protect your child, the CPSC developed these guidelines on crib safety. All cribs should have the following:

- **MATTRESS.** Use a firm, tight-fitting mattress so that your baby cannot get trapped between the mattress and the crib.
- **CRIB HARDWARE.** Be sure that there are no missing, loose, broken, or improperly installed screws, brackets, or other hardware on the crib or mattress support.
- **CRIB SLATS.** There shouldn't be more than 2 3/8 inches between the crib slats so that your baby's body cannot fit through the slats. There also shouldn't be any missing or cracked slats.
- **CRIB POSTS.** Check that your child's crib doesn't have any corner posts over 1/16 inch high so that your baby's clothing cannot get caught and lead to strangulation.
- **NO CUTOUTS.** Your child's crib shouldn't have any cutouts in the headboard or footboard so that baby's head cannot get trapped.
- **MANUFACTURED SINCE 1990.** Only use a crib that has been manufactured since 1990 and has been certified to meet national safety standards. These cribs will have

a Juvenile Products Manufacturers label. If you have
a used crib that does not have this label or is not safe,
don't use it.

Co-sleeping

YOU NEED TO decide for yourself if you want your baby to
sleep with you, whether that is in your bed or in your bedroom.
Co-sleeping is very common, especially in the first few months.
A recent study in the United States found that although only 7
percent of parents had planned on it, almost half of all parents
shared a bed with their 1-month-old baby. By three months, 28
percent of parents were still sharing a bed with their baby. This
practice clearly varies by culture, with almost all babies in many
countries sharing a bed with their parents. It is, obviously, less
common in the United States.

Interestingly, it depends on the age of your baby as to whether sharing a bed with your baby helps or hurts *your* sleep. One
study found that parents felt less fatigued if their baby slept in
their bed at 1 month of age. However, at 3 months of age, parents felt more fatigued if their baby was still sharing their bed.

Parents sleep with their babies in the same bed or same room
for many different reasons. One is as a lifestyle choice; you may
think that it is important to have your baby close by you during the night. Another reason is that you may not have another
choice, whether that is because you have a small home, are living
with your parents, or are not ready to put a newborn in the same
room with your older child.

Other parents sleep with their child as a way to solve sleep
issues. They are tired of getting up throughout the night, so
finally they just put their baby in bed with them. For these

families, making changes to encourage their child to sleep elsewhere is worthwhile.

No matter why you are sharing a bed or a room with your baby, there are several things that you should consider:

MAKE SURE THAT IT IS SAFE. The American Academy of Pediatrics, as mentioned above, has recommended that parents do not share a bed with their baby, as it can increase the risk of SIDS. A better choice is to use a bassinet or sidecar sleeper, which attaches to your bed.

MAKE SURE THAT EVERYONE AGREES. If there is more than one parent in your home, make sure that everyone agrees with the sleeping arrangements. Your baby should bring joy to both of you, not cause any frustration or resentment.

MAKE SURE THAT EVERYONE IS GETTING ENOUGH SLEEP. Whether or not you co-sleep with your baby, and this may be either sharing a room or a bed, you may not be getting as much sleep as you would otherwise. After two months of age, moms who co-sleep often get less overall sleep and are usually awake more often during the night. Your baby may also get less overall sleep and wake more often during the night. Be sure to establish good sleep habits for your baby if you are co-sleeping, just as you would if your baby were sleeping in another room. This will help everyone get plenty of sleep.

Coping with Day/Night Reversal

SOME BABIES ARE night owls, with their days and nights reversed. These babies sleep much of the day and then are awake at night. In fact, during the day, things may seem easy. Your baby sleeps much of the time, wakes to feed, plays a little, and goes back to sleep. However, at night she's up for hours, right when it's time for you to finally get some rest.

WHAT YOU CAN DO. During the first week or two, there is not much that you can do. You may have to become a night owl yourself for the time being. Once your baby is 1 to 3 weeks old, however, there are things that you can do to help get her clock on track. During the day, when she is awake, play with her as much as you can. Wake her for daytime feedings, even if she seems to be sleeping soundly. Don't try to stay quiet all the time. Be your usual noisy daytime self. And, most important, expose her to light. Keep the shades open in her room. Hang out with her in the brightest room in your house. Head outside and go for a walk, especially in the morning. Light is one of the strongest cues to helping your baby be awake more during the day and sleep better at night.

During the night, play very little with her. Keep her room dark. Turn on only a nightlight or low light for feedings and diaper changes. Be quiet and soothing. Move in slow motion. Basically, be as boring as possible. Within a week or two, your little night owl will switch around, learning that daytime is for fun and nighttime is for sleeping.

Colic

Francesca and Ted were losing their minds. Their daughter Clare, who was just 7 weeks old, screamed every day starting around 4:00 in the afternoon. The crying was incessant and they couldn't ever figure out what was wrong. Clare would finally fall asleep around 11:00 at night, after exhausting herself and her parents.

Colic equals tough times for parents. Between 10 and 25 percent of babies develop colic, defined as excessive crying that occurs during the first three months of life in an otherwise healthy baby. The crying of a baby with colic is usually unrelenting. Most pediatricians use the "rule of threes" to diagnose colic: a baby cries for three hours at a time, three days a week, for at least three weeks. Colic is usually not diagnosed until at least 3 weeks of age, and it peaks at 6 weeks of age. Then, around 3 months, babies with colic will seem miraculously cured. No one is certain what causes colic, and the cause is likely different for individual babies. For example, it may be related to an immature digestive system or a still-developing nervous system.

Colic not only involves lots of crying, but it can also disrupt sleep. Babies with colic sleep less during the night and wake more frequently—not exactly what you need after dealing with a crying baby all day. Colicky babies are also more restless when they sleep. During the day it is harder to tell when they will nap and for how long. So parents of babies with colic are not only sleep deprived, but it is also much more difficult for them to get other things done when the baby is sleeping, because it is hard to predict when their baby will wake up.

WHAT YOU CAN DO. Researchers do not know for sure the cause of colic, and there is no known cure or treatment. But this doesn't mean you can't try. Talk to your doctor about ways to help your baby. Change your diet if you are nursing, or your baby's formula if she's bottle-fed. Try swaddling your baby or putting him in a vibrating seat. A pacifier can soothe some colicky babies, whereas others do best with a change in scenery, such as going for a walk outside or a drive in the car. Your attempts may not work or may work only some of the time, but doing nothing can be even more stressful.

Be sure to also take care of yourself. Try to get through this period while maintaining your sanity. You'll need help and you'll need to get away from the situation. Take a walk, head out for a drive or to the store, and beg every friend and family member you have to watch the baby for even just a few minutes.

Sleep and Breast-feeding

Rayna was still up every two hours feeding Amber, who was now 4 months old. She had expected to be feeding her this often during the first month or two, but couldn't believe that Amber still needed such frequent feedings. It had gotten to the point where Amber could only fall asleep while nursing and no one else could put Amber to bed. Rayna realized that it was time to make some changes.

ONE OF THE surprises of nursing that may fall in the category of "no one ever told me" is that breast-fed babies often sleep for shorter periods and are usually older when they finally begin to sleep through the night. This is not the case for every baby, but rather is a general rule.

There are several reasons that breast-fed babies may sleep for shorter periods. First, breast milk is much easier for babies to digest than formula, which means shorter intervals between feedings. So a baby at 8 weeks may still be breast-feeding every 2 or 3 hours throughout the night, while a formula-fed baby may be sleeping for up to 4 to 6 hours a night. Second, breast-fed babies are more likely to fall asleep while feeding and thus may quickly develop the habit of being able to fall asleep only while nursing. This means that when your baby naturally wakes up during the night, she'll need to be nursed back to sleep.

WHAT YOU CAN DO. Babies who are breast-fed can definitely become champion sleepers. The key is to avoid falling into the trap of nursing your baby to sleep (although it is quite tempting). Instead, nurse your baby earlier in her bedtime routine. Nurse, and then wash up, change into pajamas, and sing lullabies. Even better, nurse somewhere else in the house and then head to the bedroom for your baby's bedtime routine. Be consistent about putting your baby down drowsy but awake. Having the ability to soothe herself to sleep means that your baby will naturally start sleeping for longer stretches when she no longer needs the frequent nighttime feedings.

Does this mean that you can't ever nurse your baby to sleep? Of course not. There are times when you will need to nurse your baby to sleep, especially when she is sick or extra fussy. However, you want it to be the exception rather than the norm.

Finally, I can attest to the importance of separating nursing from sleep. I nursed my own daughter until she was 20 months old, but I always put her down awake at bedtime and for naps from a very young age. She was a great sleeper, other than the usual bumps along the way, such as when she was ill or when she decided that pulling herself up to standing was much more fun than sleeping.

Swaddle Your Newborn

MANY NEWBORNS SLEEP much better swaddled. The tight feeling is reassuring and comforting. In addition, swaddling your baby will reduce the likelihood that she will wake up when she startles.

Manage Feedings to Maximize Sleep

MOST BABIES WHO are healthy and growing no longer need nighttime feedings after 6 months of age. Many babies, though, can go all night without a feeding at an even younger age. This leads to a common dilemma for moms, trying to figure out whether their baby is actually hungry at night and needs to be fed or is just waking out of habit. If your baby is hungry, obviously you want to feed her. However, if it's just a habit, then you may want to make some changes, especially working on getting her to learn to soothe herself to sleep.

You may also want to make some changes in your baby's feeding schedule to help maximize sleep at night.

Add a Dream Feeding

Try adding a dream feeding around 10:30 to 11:30 at night, before you or your husband head to bed. Some refer to this as a scheduled feeding or a focal feeding. One of the worst feelings in the world is to happily drift off to sleep at 11:00 at night, only to be awakened by your baby a half hour later. Instead, wake your baby to feed him before you go to bed. You will be surprised as to how well this works. He'll likely barely wake up but will happily eat. Both of you can then sleep soundly for 3 to 4 hours before the next feeding.

Add a Daytime Feeding

Making changes in your child's daytime feeding schedule may also help your child sleep better at night. For example, you can try moving your baby's feedings closer together during the day to fit in an extra feeding. This can help your baby get the nutrition he needs during the day, making nighttime feedings less necessary. So if your baby is eating every 3.5 hours, try every 3 hours instead. This will fit in an extra feeding during the day, which may decrease your baby's need for one of his nighttime feedings.

Manage Nighttime Feedings

There are also some things that you can do to help with nighttime feedings. First of all, be quiet and boring during nighttime feedings. You don't want to encourage your baby to wake up for fun and games in the middle of the night. Keep lights dim or just turn on a nightlight. If your baby can't seem to go more than an hour or two between night feedings, you can also try gradually lengthening the time between feedings to help him sleep longer.

Pacifiers: The Great Debate

MANY PARENTS STRUGGLE with trying to decide whether to let their baby use a pacifier. Some parents do not like the idea of their baby having a pacifier in her mouth all the time and are concerned about establishing a habit that they will have to change at some point. Some babies, however, have a strong need to suck and find a pacifier to be very soothing, whereas other babies have no interest in a pacifier and will keep spitting it out. If you decide to give your baby a pacifier, be sure to wait until breast-feeding is well established if you are nursing, as giving a pacifier too early can cause nipple confusion. Another important piece of information is that the American Academy of Pediatrics has recently come out with a statement that pacifier use may decrease the risk of SIDS.

Babies who use pacifiers are great sleepers, but that is not until your baby is about 6 months old. Before that age, your baby will need her pacifier to fall asleep at bedtime and every time she naturally wakes up at night, but unfortunately she won't be able to get her pacifier on her own. She'll need your help. This means that during the night you'll likely be getting up to give your baby back her pacifier. Once she is able to find her pacifier though, around 6 or 7 months, she'll end up being a great sleeper!

Establish Good Sleep Habits Early

Once your baby is 6 to 8 weeks old, and definitely by 3 months, it is time to start establishing good sleep habits. There are some things you can try even as young as 2 or 3 weeks. By starting early, you will help your baby sleep through the night at a very young age and prevent future sleep problems. It is so much easier to prevent sleep problems than it is to have to do sleep training when your baby is 6 months, a year, or even 2 years old. If this is your second child, you know how true this is.

By 3 months, your baby is physiologically at the point when she is able to sleep for longer stretches of time. This is also one of the easiest times to encourage good sleep habits from a developmental perspective. She can't climb out of her crib yet. Developmental milestones that can interfere with sleep, such as rolling over and separation anxiety, haven't started and poor sleep habits haven't become ingrained. Once your baby gets older—that is, at 5 or 6 months—the process of getting your baby on a sleep schedule and to sleep through the night gets more difficult. And finally, you are probably at the point where you are ready to get more than 3 or 4 continuous hours of sleep.

The First Time Your Baby Sleeps Through the Night

"The first time that I woke up at five in the morning and realized that Chloe never woke me up during the night, I was sure she was dead! I ran into her room and was amazed to see her peacefully sleeping. I checked to make sure that she was still breathing."

—Gretchen

There are several key things that you should do to help your baby become a great sleeper.

LEARN YOUR BABY'S SIGNS OF BEING TIRED. By 6 to 8 weeks of age, expect to put your child down to sleep after she has been up for about 2 hours. This is about a baby's limit at this age for how long she will be awake happy and alert. Start to look for signs that your baby is getting tired, such as rubbing her eyes, pulling on her ear, or getting fussy. The minute that you see she is tired, it's time for a nap or bedtime. Don't wait too long. If you miss your window of opportunity, she will become overtired and actually have a harder time settling down and falling asleep.

SLEEP SCHEDULE. Begin establishing a sleep schedule. This schedule should include a set bedtime, a set wake time, and set naptimes (either at set times during the day or after your baby has been awake for 2 hours). A consistent feeding schedule will also help set a more general daily routine.

BEDTIME AND NAPTIME ROUTINES. Even starting at 2 or 3 weeks, your baby will benefit from a bedtime routine and a naptime routine. At this age, it may be as simple as a sponge bath, diaper change, pajamas, and a lullaby at bedtime, and just a diaper change and lullaby at naptimes. Your bedtime routine may only take 5 minutes, but it will signal to your baby that it is sleep time. By 3 to 6 months, your bedtime routine may take 30 to 45 minutes. It should be the same three to four activities in the same order every night, such as a bath, massage, and stories.

PUT YOUR BABY DOWN DROWSY BUT AWAKE. Babies need to be able to put themselves to sleep without your intervention. The reason is that all babies wake up two to six times during the night. This is normal. Waking up at night is not what's problematic, but rather the inability to return to sleep. When your baby has learned to soothe herself to sleep, she can then immediately do so after she naturally awakens. In contrast, if you nurse your baby to sleep at bedtime, you'll be nursing her back to sleep every time she wakes up during the night. If you rock her to sleep, you'll be rocking her back to sleep.

By 3 months of age, start putting your baby down when she is still awake. For some babies, you can even do this right from the beginning. When your baby is very young, (less than 3 months) consider these practice sessions. Babies this young should not be left to cry for a prolonged period. Put her down, say "night-night," leave, and see what happens. If your baby starts to whimper and fuss, wait a few minutes. She may quickly settle down and fall asleep. If she starts to get very upset, go and get her and do whatever you normally do to help her fall asleep. Wait until the next sleep time or another day and try again. Often parents are stunned by their baby's self-soothing abilities. Many babies are happy to be put down, look at their favorite toy, and drift off to sleep on their own.

Walk, Don't Run

DURING THE NIGHT when you hear your baby begin to stir, walk, don't run to him. You will be surprised how often he'll fall back to sleep on his own. Remember, all babies naturally wake up throughout the night. Your baby may simply be stirring, ready to return right back to sleep. By going to him too quickly, you may actually be waking him up.

The more practice that your baby gets putting herself to sleep, the quicker the process works. She will fall asleep on her own, and she will get the sleep that she needs. Again, don't wait too long to start putting your baby down awake. The earlier, the better.

Putting your baby down awake is the key to getting babies to sleep through the night from an early age!

SLEEP TRAINING. At some point, you may need to encourage your child to learn to fall asleep on her own if she hasn't taken to it with practice sessions. Yes, this is the hard part. It depends on your child, but you can begin sleep training anytime between 3 and 6 months of age. At this age, your baby will be ready to develop self-soothing skills.

So how do you do this? After your child's bedtime routine, say good night, and leave the room. Don't nurse him. Don't let him fall asleep in the living room. Don't stay with him. Your child is likely to be upset by the change in his routine. Wait. Then do a simple checking routine.

Go back into your child's room. Tell him that you love him and that it is night-night time. Pat him or touch him if you wish. If you need to, you can even pick him up briefly, although this can end up prolonging the process for some babies. Remain fairly neutral and stay for a short time, no more than 1 minute. Basically, make the visits brief and boring.

Leave. Wait again. Check again. Repeatedly wait and then check on your child, as frequently or infrequently as you wish. It actually doesn't matter whether you wait 30 seconds or 10 minutes. How often you check on your child will depend on your baby's temperament and your tolerance. All you want is to catch that golden moment when your child falls asleep on his own. Expect your child to be upset for about 45 minutes the first night, about an hour or a bit more the second night (it always gets worse before it gets better), and a much shorter time from the third night on.

It is recommended that you first focus on bedtime only. Keep doing whatever you normally do when your baby wakes at night—feel free to nurse her or rock her back to sleep. Most babies naturally start sleeping for longer and longer stretches at night once they are able to fall asleep on their own, which usually happens within two weeks of them falling asleep quickly and easily at bedtime. Therefore, there is usually no reason to also do sleep training during the night.

However, if by 6 months of age your baby is still waking during the night, you might want to start middle-of-the-night sleep training. At that point, your baby will likely no longer need nighttime feedings and he'll hopefully be well on his way to being able to find his pacifier if he uses one.

Maria and Robert decided it was time to make some changes. Their son Noah, at 5 months, was still waking two or three times every night. The only way to get him back to sleep was for Maria to nurse him. They decided to start putting Noah down awake at bedtime rather than Maria nursing him to sleep. Since it was especially hard on Robert to hear Noah cry, Maria waited until Robert was out of town. The first night was not as difficult as she expected. Noah only cried for 20 minutes. The second and third night he cried for 40 minutes and Maria was discouraged. On the fourth night, though, she was stunned when he fell asleep within 5 minutes and actually slept for 6 hours straight. It was the first time ever! From that night on, Noah began falling asleep with no problem at bedtime and sleeping for longer and longer stretches.

Twins, Triplets . . . or More

TWINS CAN DEFINITELY be twice as much fun. They also can be twice as much work. Managing sleep with twins (or more) is critical, or else you will never get any sleep. A few essentials when it comes to twins:

- **SHARING NIGHTTIME DUTY.** Sharing nighttime duty is even more important when you have twins. There is no way that you'll be able to see straight if you are up throughout the night and then are taking care of twins all day long. Split nighttime duty with Dad as best that you can. This may mean each of you responsible for one twin or each of you taking turns.
- **GET NIGHTTIME HELP.** Even if you have two parents in your home, getting extra help at night, even if just once in a while, will help tremendously.
- **PUT THEM ON THE SAME SLEEP SCHEDULE.** Be sure and keep your twins on the same schedule. That means synchronizing sleep and feeding schedules. Put both down at bedtime and for naps at the same time. If one wakes to feed during the night, wake the other.
- **GIVE YOURSELF PLENTY OF TIME.** Everything takes longer with twins (or more), so be sure and set aside plenty of time at bedtime to get everyone ready for bed.
- **ESTABLISH SLEEP HABITS SUPER EARLY.** It's hard enough to have one 6-month-old waking twice at night; it's worse to have two or three of them doing it. From early on, be sure to help your babies learn to self-soothe to sleep. This may mean a few tears at the moment, but definitely less tears in the long run.

Make Sleep Transitions by 3 Months

IN THE FIRST few weeks to months, many parents have their babies sleep in a bassinet, infant seat, or other smaller space. The crib often seems too huge for such a tiny baby, and a bassinet can easily be set up in the parents' bedroom. If you plan to have your baby eventually sleep in a crib, you need to make the transition by 3 months. Wait much longer than 3 months and it will be much more difficult for your baby. After 3 months, habits are set and the change in sleeping location will feel too new and different.

When you start the transition, you can do it all at once or gradually. For a gradual change, start with just naps or just bedtime in the crib. Once your baby is used to the new location, move on to napping and sleeping in the crib all night. Some babies do much better in the crib if you put them down in a corner of the crib, rather than in the middle. Having one of their sides and their head up against the crib bumpers may help them feel more secure. Putting rolled-up receiving blankets on all sides of your baby will also do the trick.

The same is true about how your baby falls asleep. If you want to be rocking her to sleep when she is a year old, then feel free to continue to do so. But if your image is to put her down at bedtime and naptime, with her falling asleep on her own, make the change now.

Top Sleep Tips Revisited

IN CASE YOU slept through your reading of them the first time, here are the top sleep tips to help your baby sleep through the night.

1. **SET BEDTIME AND NAPTIMES.** Make sure that your baby is going to bed at a set bedtime, and make sure that it is early enough. If you put your baby to bed too late, he will be over-tired and will have a harder time falling asleep and staying asleep. Also, by having a set bedtime, your baby's body will learn to be tired at the same time every night. The same is true for naps; taking a nap at the same time will help your baby fall asleep easier.

2. **BEDTIME ROUTINE.** Starting at a very young age, develop a consistent bedtime routine that includes the same three or four activities in the same order. For a newborn, it may be washing up, changing into pajamas, and a lullaby. For an older infant, it may be taking a bath, changing into pajamas, and listening to two stories. A bedtime routine is a great way to transition from a busy day to winding down for sleep. It will also be a wonderful time that you share with your baby.

3. **PUT YOUR BABY TO BED DROWSY BUT AWAKE.** You want to be sure that your baby is able to self-soothe to sleep. All infants naturally wake up throughout the night. If your baby can fall asleep on her own at bedtime, she'll be able to fall back asleep on her own throughout the night. If, instead, you rock or nurse your baby to sleep at bedtime, you will need to rock or nurse her back to sleep every time she naturally wakes up.

And One Final Piece of Advice—Savor the Moments

TALK TO ANY mom of a child over the age of 3, when she has a 4-year-old, a 9-year-old, or a 15-year-old, and you'll hear the exact same thing over and over: "It goes so fast." It really does. When you are home with a baby and it seems as if she's crying nonstop for days and days or nights and nights, it may feel like it will never end. You will be surprised, though, how quickly it all really does goes by.

So be sure to savor the moments. Slow down and enjoy the wonderful times—snuggling with your baby, watching her discover her toes for the first time, or even just staring at her and trying to figure out who she looks like. No matter how tired you are, take a deep breath, stop, and enjoy the moments. At the end of the day, write down one or two endearing things that your baby did. When you are at your most sleep deprived, you can go and read it to help keep you going.

Savor other moments, too. Enjoy the first sip of your morning coffee while watching the sun come up on a new day. Check out the changing color of the leaves while driving to the grocery store. Stop and literally smell a flower.

Will this make you feel less sleep deprived? Probably not, but it will help you feel more centered and calmer about life.

Reminders

- Be realistic. Every baby is different.
- Most babies need nighttime feedings the first few months, but few rarely do after 6 months.

- Establish a safe sleeping environment for your baby, including ensuring that your baby sleeps in a safe place and on her back.
- Swaddling and managing feedings can both maximize sleep.
- Establishing good sleep habits will help your baby start sleeping great from an early age. The three key things are developing a sleep schedule, establishing a bedtime routine, and putting your baby to bed drowsy but awake.
- And finally, enjoy every moment with your baby and being a new mom.

Appendix A:
Your Sleep Diary

Sleep Diary

EVERY MORNING WHEN you get up, complete the sleep diary for the previous night.

Day	Last night I went to bed at:	This morning I woke up at:	It took me ____ minutes to fall asleep:	Total amount of sleep:
EXAMPLE:				
Sunday	11:15	6:20	25	6h 40min
____	____	____	____	____
____	____	____	____	____
____	____	____	____	____
____	____	____	____	____
____	____	____	____	____
____	____	____	____	____

Appendix B

Resources

Books

PARENTING BOOKS

Sleeping Through the Night: How Infants, Toddlers, and Their Parents Can Get a Good Night's Sleep (rev. ed.)
Jodi A. Mindell, Ph.D.

Caring for Your Baby and Young Child: Birth to Age 5
American Academy of Pediatrics

Touchpoints: Birth to Three: Your Child's Emotional and Behavioral Development
T. Berry Brazelton, M.D., and Joshua D. Sparrow, M.D.

What to Expect the First Year
Arlene Eisenberg, Heidi E. Murkoff, and Sandee E. Hathaway

ADULT SLEEP

The Promise of Sleep: A Pioneer in Sleep Medicine Explores the Vital Connection Between Health, Happiness, and a Good Night's Sleep
William C. Dement, M.D., Ph.D.

Power Sleep: The Revolutionary Program That Prepares Your Mind for Peak Performance
James Maas, Ph.D., et al.

No More Sleepless Nights
Peter Hauri, Ph.D., and Shirley Linde, Ph.D.

A Woman's Guide to Sleep Disorders
Meir Kryger, M.D.

A Woman's Guide to Sleep: Guaranteed Solutions for a Good Night's Rest
Joyce Walsleben, Ph.D., and Rita Baron-Faust

The Woman's Book of Sleep: A Complete Resource Guide
Amy Wolfson, Ph.D.

POSTPARTUM DEPRESSION

Down Came the Rain: My Journey Through Postpartum Depression
Brooke Shields

This Isn't What I Expected: Overcoming Postpartum Depression
Karen Kleiman, M.S.W., and Valerie Raskin, M.D.

Conquering Postpartum Depression
Ronald Rosenberg, M.D., Deborah Greening, Ph.D., and
James Windell, M.A.

*Beyond the Blues: A Guide to Understanding and Treating
Prenatal and Postpartum Depression*
Shoshana S. Bennett, Ph.D., and Pec Indman, Ed.D.

BED REST

Days in Waiting: A Guide to Surviving Pregnancy Bed Rest
(2nd ed.)
Mary Ann McCann

*The Pregnancy Bed Rest Book: A Survival Guide for Expectant
Mothers and Their Families*
Amy E. Tracy

Pregnancy Bedrest: A Journey of Love
Wanda Hale

Organizations and Resources

POSTPARTUM DEPRESSION
Postpartum Support International (PSI)
927 North Kellogg Avenue
Santa Barbara, CA 93111
(800) 944–4PPD
postpartum.net

Postpartum Progress
postpartumprogress.typepad.com

Postpartum Stress Center
postpartumstress.com

HIGH-RISK PREGNANCIES AND BED REST

Sidelines
National High Risk Pregnancy Support Network
P. O. Box 1808
Laguna Beach, CA 92652
(888) 447–4754 (HI-RISK4)
sidelines.org

SIDS

National SIDS/Infant Death Resource Center
2070 Chain Bridge Road, Suite 450
Vienna, VA 22182
(866) 866–7437
sidscenter.org

SIDS Alliance
1314 Bedford Avenue, Suite 210
Baltimore, MD 21208
(410) 653–8226
sidsalliance.com

TWINS AND MORE GROUPS

National Organization of Mothers of Twins Clubs
(NOMOTC)
P.O. Box 438
Thompsons Station, TN 37179
(877) 540-2200
nomotc.org

Mothers of Supertwins
P.O. Box 306
East Islip, NY 11730
(631) 859-1110
mostonline.org

BREAST-FEEDING

La Leche League International
1400 North Meacham Road
Schaumburg, Il 60173-4808
(847) 519-7730
(800) 525-3243
lalecheleague.org

GENERAL PARENTING WEBSITES

BabyCenter.com
Parents.com
Johnsonsbaby.com/sleep

SLEEP

National Sleep Foundation (NSF)
1522 K Street, N.W., Suite 500
Washington, DC 20005
(202) 341–3471
sleepfoundation.org

American Academy of Sleep Medicine (AASM)
One Westbrook Corporate Center, Suite 920
Westchester, IL 60154
(708) 492–0930
aasmnet.org
sleepeducation.com
sleepcenters.org
americaninsomniaassociation.org

Sleep Research Society
One Westbrook Corporate Center
Suite 920
Westchester, IL 60154
(708) 492–0930
sleepresearchsociety.org

Narcolepsy Network Inc.
10921 Reed Hartman Highway
Cincinnati, OH 45242
(513) 891–3522
narcolepsynetwork.org

Restless Legs Syndrome Foundation
819 Second Street, S.W.
Rochester, MN 55902–2985
rls.org

American Sleep Apnea Association
A.W.A.K.E. Network
1424 K Street, N.W., Suite 302
Washington, DC 20005
(202) 293–3650
sleepapnea.org

Index